A COLLECT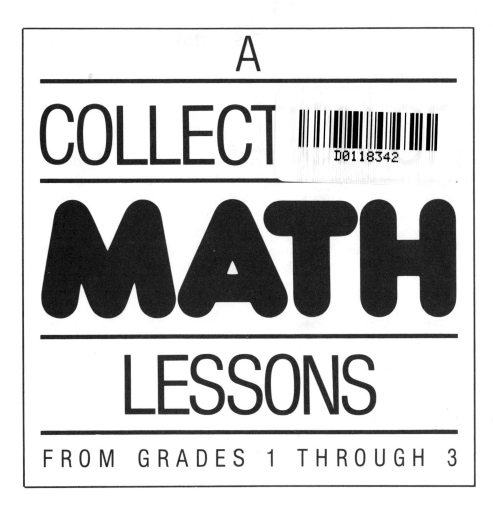 MATH LESSONS

FROM GRADES 1 THROUGH 3

BY MARILYN BURNS
AND BONNIE TANK

MATH SOLUTIONS PUBLICATIONS

ACKNOWLEDGMENTS

Special thanks to the teachers and children in whose classes the lessons were taught.

Christine Brinkley, Carlinville School District, Illinois
Barbara Buckley, Bellevue Public Schools, Washington
Varien Gacek, Bellevue Public Schools, Washington
Marge Genolio, San Francisco Unified School District, California
Pat Granucci, San Francisco Unified School District, California
Gloria Mitchell, Bellevue Public Schools, Washington
Leslie Salkeld, Edison School District, Washington
Marge Tsukamoto, San Francisco Unified School District, California
Dee Uyeda, Mill Valley Public Schools, California

Math Solutions Publications
A division of
Marilyn Burns Education Associates
150 Gate 5 Road, Suite 101
Sausalito, CA 94965
www.mathsolutions.com

Telephone: (800) 868-9092 or (415) 332-4181
Fax: (415) 331-1931

ISBN 0-941355-01-2

Art Direction and Design: William S. Wells
Layout and Production: Jean McLean
Typography: Hillside Setting
Editing: Barbara Youngblood
Illustration: Martha Weston

Printed in the United States of America

Available on Videotape
Some lessons from each book in the *Collection of Math Lessons* series have been captured on three series of videotapes—*Mathematics with Manipulatives* (K–6), *Mathematics: Teaching for Understanding* (K–6), and *Mathematics for Middle School* (6–8). Classes of elementary and middle school students are taught by Marilyn Burns and other Math Solutions instructors.

The videotapes are available from Math Solutions Publications, 150 Gate 5 Road, Suite 101, Sausalito, CA 94965. For information, telephone (800) 868-9092.

A Message from Marilyn Burns

We at Marilyn Burns Education Associates believe that teaching mathematics well calls for increasing our understanding of the math we teach, seeking greater insight into how children learn mathematics, and refining lessons to best promote children's learning. Math Solutions helps teachers achieve these goals by providing professional development through inservice courses and publications.

Our publications include a wide range of choices, from books in our new Teaching Arithmetic and Lessons for Algebraic Thinking series to resources that link math and literacy; from books to help teachers understand mathematics more deeply to children's books that help students develop an appreciation for math while learning basic concepts.

Our inservice programs offer five-day courses, one-day workshops, and series of school-year sessions throughout the country, working in partnership with school districts to help implement and sustain long-term improvement in mathematics instruction in all classrooms.

To find a complete listing of our publications and workshops, please visit our Web site at *www.mathsolutions.com*. Or contact us by calling (800) 868-9092 or sending an e-mail to *info@mathsolutions.com*.

We're eager for your feedback and interested in learning about your particular needs. We look forward to hearing from you.

A DIVISION OF MARILYN BURNS EDUCATION ASSOCIATES

CONTENTS

Introduction

> About Mathematics
>
> When I think about mathematics I think about learning and deciding if I should keep rolling the dice or if I should keep my score in the game of pig. I also think about which number would get to the top first in the game of two spiner-sums.
> I think about what rods can be made out of two other rods of the same color.

"When you think about mathematics, what do you think about?" we asked a class of third graders. Several hands shot up immediately, and in the course of the discussion almost all the children had something to say.

"It's numbers."

"It's when you add two numbers."

"It's when you make numbers bigger."

"It's odd and even."

"Sometimes you do take away."

One child said, "When I think of math, I think YUK!" After a moment, however, he qualified his comment, "No, just subtraction."

Common to all children's responses was that mathematics involves number. Also common was that mathematics is isolated from the real world and has no particular purpose or usefulness.

After experiencing many of the lessons in this book, we asked the third graders the same question. This time they wrote their responses. Most of their comments again included references to number and especially to adding and subtracting. But they also included much more.

"When I think about mathematics I think about looking at money when I go to 7-11 and adding how much there is. About subtracting a special year from 1987 to find out how long ago it was."

"I think about thinking because you have to think when you do math."

"When I think about mathematics I think about learning and deciding if I should keep rolling the dice or if I should keep my score in the game of pig."

"I think about when they first made the counting blocks."

"When I think about mathematics I think about writing, explaining, adding, subtracting, using materials, understanding more about mathematics, and using your head."

"When I think about mathematics, I think about fun, learning, and sharing."

The premise of this book is that the emphasis of math instruction should be on helping children learn to think and reason mathematically. Children should approach mathematics with a view toward its usefulness. They should be presented with problems to solve that require them to use concepts and skills they have learned and to help them bring meaning to those concepts they do not yet understand.

The traditional goal of mathematics instruction for the primary grades has been to help young children develop understanding of number concepts and skills. More specifically, it is arithmetic that is central to math teaching in the early grades. Children's math experiences focus on mastering basic facts, learning and practicing the skills of addition and subtraction with and without regrouping, and then moving on to multiplication and division. Because being able to do arithmetic is the prevalent measure of children's math success, children spend the bulk of math time doing paper-and-pencil arithmetic exercises.

In the lessons in this book, however, it is doing mathematics, rather than doing arithmetic, that gets primary attention. Children are involved in sorting, classifying, making graphs, exploring geometric relationships, measuring, applying logical reasoning, making predictions, devising strategies, collecting, organizing, and interpreting statistical information. Children's work with arithmetic is moved off the static pages of pencil-and-paper drill into lessons in which they estimate, invent algorithmic procedures, and use numbers in problem-solving situations.

ABOUT THE LESSONS IN THIS BOOK

The lessons presented in this book represent years of work with children. Each lesson was taught to several classes, often at different grade levels and at different times in the school year. We tinkered with the lessons. We discussed children's responses, revised plans, changed sequences, and tried the lessons over and over again. What we've presented is the best of what we learned from our experiences.

When creating lessons for children, we kept five principles in mind.

1. Lessons were to be built around problem-solving experiences that require children to think and reason.

2. Lessons would deal with important mathematics concepts to help children develop and extend their understanding of mathematics.

3. Children would be encouraged to talk with one another about their ideas during lessons and to describe their thoughts in writing.

4. Whenever appropriate, children were to use concrete materials to solve problems and to help them bring meaning to abstract concepts.

5. Children would be organized into small groups to work together cooperatively, giving them opportunities to verbalize their thoughts, clarify their ideas, get reactions from others, and listen to others' points of view.

The lessons we taught varied in length. Some were taught in one class period; others required a period of several days; longer lessons involved children for a week or more. Sometimes a lesson expanded when an activity suggested extensions that provided explorations for the children for several additional days.

We found that it was not easy to plan accurately the amount of time a lesson would require. We found that the same lesson took different amounts of time with different classes and at different grade levels. This did not trouble us. As long as children were motivated and involved with the mathematics they were exploring, we continued. Too often, it is the timetable of the curriculum that pushes children's learning instead of the children's mathematics abilities and interests.

The lessons in this book deal with a variety of topics. Some are standard to primary math programs—place value, addition, and beginning division, for example. Other topics generally receive less attention in grades 1 through 3—ratio and proportion, symmetry, and probability. In many of the lessons, concepts from more than one area of mathematics are interwoven to help children see the interrelatedness of mathematical ideas.

All lessons are written as vignettes to help provide the flavor of what actually occurred with children. Each vignette begins with an introduction that describes the lesson and provides a rationale. Along with the classroom scenario, samples of children's work are included, some as part of the text and others reproduced in the children's own handwriting. In both cases, the children's misspellings and grammatical errors have not been corrected, and their work appears unedited.

THE USE OF MANIPULATIVE MATERIALS

Manipulative materials are used in most lessons in the book. Using manipulative materials is not a new notion in education; they have long been available to schools. A sizable body of research attests to the value of materials for helping children bring meaning to mathematical concepts.

Manipulative materials help children think and reflect about mathematical ideas. Materials help children develop understanding of new concepts and relate new concepts to what they have already learned. They assist with the solving of problems. They provide tactile and visual opportunities for seeing mathematical relationships. Without manipulative materials, children are too often lost in a world of abstract symbols for which they have no concrete connection or comprehension.

A variety of concrete objects are used in the lessons in this book. Some of the materials we used are available at home or at local markets—macaroni, toothpicks, marbles, dice, beans, popcorn, lentils, boxes of various sizes. We also used commercially produced educational materials—Unifix cubes, Cuisenaire Rods, Base Ten Blocks, Color Tiles.

Unifix cubes are interlocking cubes, made in ten colors, that children can easily snap into trains. Cuisenaire Rods are made in ten lengths, from one centimeter to ten centimeters; each rod length is a different color. Base Ten Blocks provide a model of our place-value system and are made in unit cubes, tens rods, hundreds squares, and thousands blocks. Color Tiles are one-inch-square tiles made in four colors. Each of these materials has a variety of uses in the lessons. (Please note that the materials used in these lessons do not reflect all that is available or appropriate for young children. There are many others that are also suitable and that provide exciting ways for children to explore mathematical concepts.)

It is important to keep in mind that whenever a material is introduced in the classroom, children need time to explore it before being asked to use it in a particular lesson. It is difficult, even impossible, to focus young children's attention on a specific activity when they are intrigued and curious about a material. In this case, the material will be more of a distraction than an assist to learning.

ORGANIZING THE CLASS FOR COOPERATIVE LEARNING

In all lessons, children work together in small groups. They are encouraged to work cooperatively and to explain their ideas, to listen and question one another, and to agree on solutions. When children are in small groups, they have more opportunities to express their thoughts than in whole-class discussions. Also, they may be more comfortable trying out their thinking in the setting of a small group than before an entire class.

The sizes of the groups we used varied. Sometimes children worked in pairs; at other times groups were made up of three or four children; in one lesson children worked in groups of six. In groups of any size, children were expected to work together so that everyone in the group was involved, contributing, and understanding.

Seating children together does not necessarily insure that children will work together effectively. They need to understand that they are all expected to participate and to encourage their group members to participate.

Problems arose in some lessons when children were learning to work cooperatively. Children had disputes about who would go first when playing games. Some groups had difficulties negotiating who would do the recording required. Sometimes one child would hog all the blocks during an activity, or a child would not be interested in participating and would play instead. We dealt with situations such as those by talking with groups when difficulties arose and by having class discussions about general problems.

The problem behaviors we experienced were not very different from problems that occur when children work individually. Classroom rules need to be reinforced, children need to be encouraged, alternative ways to solve problems need to be discussed. We are staunch believers that helping children learn to work cooperatively is well worth the effort. A classroom that values and promotes social interaction provides children with support that is an essential ingredient for learning.

INCORPORATING CHILDREN'S WRITING

Writing was incorporated as an integral part of math lessons, with writing assignments geared for the age level and abilities of the students. Having children write is a way to extend and deepen their thinking processes. They have the opportunity to formulate and rethink their ideas.

At times, groups collaborated when writing. If the group worked together to reach a collective solution to a problem, it made sense to have them present their solution and describe how they reached it in a group paper. At other times, however, children were given individual assignments; for example, to reflect on an experience and express their thoughts. As with all teaching decisions, there is no hard-and-fast rule to follow. It is a judgment call based on the activity, the children, and the teacher's goal.

At times, usually when first working with a class, some children were resistant to writing. "What should I write?" and "I don't know what to say" were common comments. With time and experience, children's confidence grew.

To help students, we often structured students' writing to encourage their efforts. Sometimes we wrote the beginning of a sentence on the chalkboard for the children to complete. "We think there are _____ tiles in the bag because..." "My strategy for playing is..." "The graph tells me that..." We think it takes _____ rods because..." In all cases, the goal for the writing was for children to express their thinking and reasoning processes, not merely to record answers.

We also found it useful to have groups or individuals read what they had written to the class. There were several benefits from this. Children having difficulty with their writing were provided with models. Also, having an audience seemed to encourage children to be more complete and careful when expressing their thoughts.

Having children write supports their learning. The process of writing provides children with the opportunity to reflect on what they have been doing. When children commit their thoughts to writing, they enrich, extend, and cement their learning experiences. Samples of children's responses to writing assignments are included throughout the book.

HOW TO USE THIS BOOK

The usefulness of the book will be derived, we think, from the cumulative effect of reading the seventeen chapters. Though the topics, activities, and grade levels differ, the collection of vignettes describes how lessons are introduced, how children respond, and what a teacher might do. Each chapter adds something different to the picture of what is possible in problem-solving math lessons.

The chapters have been organized into four sections—Building Number Sense, Developing Understanding of Place Value, Geometry and Measurement Experiences, and Probability Activities. However, overlaps exist in the focus of lessons. For example, Chapter 10, describing a measurement lesson in which children explore ratio, is suitable for the section on measurement or number sense. The lesson in Chapter 16 appears in the probability section, though it involves children with a place-value game. The message we have tried to convey is that mathematics is not to be viewed as a collection of separate, unrelated topics.

Choose a lesson to try with your class, one that structures in a new way an activity with which you are already familiar or one that is entirely new for you. Keep in mind that children in your classes will have responses that differ from those described. This is good, as comparing different responses will be helpful for reflecting on what occurs with your students.

There is no one way to help children learn mathematics. There is no best way for any of these lessons to be taught. Most important is that your students learn mathematics, and that you enjoy the mathematical explorations with them.

I

Building Number Sense

Developing understanding of number is the main focus of children's primary mathematics experiences. After children learn to count and recognize numerals, they are introduced to addition and subtraction. Children spend a great deal of time mastering basic addition and subtraction facts, with much of their practice involved in completing workbook pages, using flash cards, and taking timed tests. Most of their classroom math work is done individually.

The suggestions offered in this section demonstrate a very different approach to children's early number experiences. These chapters do not offer a comprehensive and sequential instructional outline for children's number experiences in the primary grades; rather, they offer a sampling of classroom lessons that model instruction where the focus is having children use numbers in problem-solving situations, and the emphasis is on children's working cooperatively and explaining their thinking and understanding.

In these lessons, students are often asked to deal with larger numbers and more advanced concepts than are typically presented in their textbooks. The emphasis of their learning is to build number sense and understanding, not to develop algorithmic proficiency.

In Chapter 1, first graders are shown how to make necklaces using two colors of macaronis in a certain pattern. After successfully making their necklaces, they are given the opportunity to make another necklace. The second time, however, they first have to figure how many macaronis they need of each color. Their method of figuring and recording reveal much about their thinking.

In Chapter 2, first and second graders are presented with situational problems to solve. An integral part of their finding solutions is to be able to explain their reasoning to their classmates.

The lesson in Chapter 3 requires second graders to apply logical reasoning to clues to help them figure what combinations of different-colored tiles are in a bag.

In Chapter 4, third graders estimate the number of scoops of beans needed to fill a jar, and then how many beans the jar holds. In this lesson, the children interpret information represented graphically, intuitively consider average, and solve a multiplication problem.

Chapter 5 presents a collection of lessons that help children develop understanding of the concept of division.

Chapter 1
Making Necklaces

In this lesson with a class of first graders, children make necklaces using two colors of macaronis in a specified pattern. After this experience, the children have the opportunity to make another necklace using the same pattern. The second time, however, the children have to figure out and record how many of each color of macaronis they need.

This lesson provides the opportunity for assessing the children's understanding of number and pattern as they make their necklaces, their problem-solving abilities as they work to figure out how many of each color of macaronis they need, and their comfort and ability with writing as they record their work and solutions. The lesson is not only enjoyable for the children, it is also helpful for becoming acquainted with their capabilities.

BEGINNING THE LESSON

I brought two pint jars of uncooked salad macaronis to the class for the children to use for stringing necklaces. I had dyed the macaronis in one jar red. (To dye the macaronis, I used red food coloring—just enough to coat the macaronis—mixed with rubbing alcohol—about a tablespoonful—and let them dry overnight.) Also I had cut string for the necklaces and had dipped one end of each piece in white glue. When dry, the end is stiffened, making it easier for children to use.

"You are going to make necklaces today," I told the children, "using some red macaronis and some white macaronis." I showed the children the two jars of macaronis I had prepared.

"There is a certain pattern I want you to use when you make your necklaces," I continued. "Watch as I make one first." I modeled making a necklace for the children, describing the pattern as I did so.

"You start with one red macaroni," I began, putting a red macaroni on the string. "Then you put on one white macaroni. Next come two red macaronis, and then another white one. Now you add three red macaronis, followed by one white one again. Next come four red and one white, then five red and one white, and finally six red and one white." I then showed them how to attach a piece of masking tape as a label for their names.

"After you do this," I concluded, "tie the two ends of your string into a knot so you can wear it as a necklace." I tied a knot and slipped my necklace over my head.

"Who remembers which color of macaroni I used first?" I asked the children.

Carmen raised her hand. "You used a red one," she said.

"That's right," I said, pointing to the first red macaroni I had put on my necklace. I wrote "1 red" on the chalkboard.

"And then what did I put on?" I asked.

Lorene answered, "A white one." I pointed to the white one on my necklace and wrote "1 white" on the chalkboard.

"And what did I do next?" I asked.

After a moment, most of the children had raised their hands. I called on Richmond. "You put on two red ones." I wrote that on the chalkboard as well.

I continued in this manner, having the children report and listing what they reported.

1 red
1 white
2 red
1 white
3 red
1 white
4 red
1 white
5 red
1 white
6 red
1 white

"Look at the pattern I've listed," I said.

Zheng immediately called out, "What kind of a pattern is that? That's no pattern!"

"It may not be a pattern that you're familiar with," I responded. "There are many different patterns."

I circled "1 white" each time it appeared in my list. "What's the same about those?" I asked.

Tine raised her hand. "They're all white," she said.

Hassan had something to add. He said, "It's always one white."

"What about the red ones?" I asked.

Several children raised their hands to respond. I called on Melissa. "It goes 1, 2, 3, 4, 5, 6," she said.

I then had the class read the pattern with me. For more than half the children in this class, English is not their first language. Every opportunity to verbalize is valuable for them, and I try to do as much of this as possible.

I then held up the two jars, one full of white and the other full of red macaronis. "How full do you think the jars will be after we all finish making our necklaces?" I asked.

Many children were eager to share what they thought. I called on Michael. He had difficulty finding words to describe what he was thinking, so I asked him to come up and show what he thought. He did so. With two fingers, he showed that about two inches would be left in each jar. "That one this much, and that one this much," he said.

"So you think they will both have about the same amount left?" I asked. Michael nodded yes.

Michael shows how much he thinks will be left in each jar.

I red
I white
2 red
I white
3 red
I white
4 red
I white
5 red
I white
6 red
I white

"Why do you think that?" I asked.

"Because I think they'll have that much," Michael said, showing again with his fingers.

Tina explained her thinking next. "This one you will have to use more," she said, pointing to the jar with the red macaronis in it. She pointed to the other jar and said, "This one you will use less."

"Why do you think that, Tina?" I asked.

"Because you use only one white each time," she answered.

Joanne had a different idea. She came up and pointed to the jar with red macaronis. "This one will be all gone," she said.

"Why do you think that?" I asked. She couldn't explain her idea.

Other children offered ideas. None of them, however, was able to explain his or her reasoning.

'There wouldn't be any red," Mark said, "and white will have this much." He indicated with his fingers that the jar would have about two inches of macaronis left in it.

"Half, half," Nancy said, pointing to each jar.

"The macaronis will be all mixed up," Mohammad said.

After all the children who wanted to had had a chance to tell their ideas, I put shallow containers of each color of macaronis on each cluster of desks and the children got to work. I hung my necklace on a hook by the door for them to use as a reference. All children completed their necklaces by the end of the class period. They seemed pleased with the results of their efforts.

EXTENDING THE LESSON

Since the children enjoyed making their necklaces, and were successful, it made sense to build on this experience. In preparation for a follow-up activity, I cut a supply of two-inch squares of construction paper in yellow, blue, green, orange, and purple. I assembled a piece of chart paper, a large marker, a glue stick, and a flat box lid for the squares. I also brought a nested set of measuring cups from home.

I had replaced all the unused red and white macaronis in the original jars. I showed the children what was left. "Which color do we have more of now?" I asked. It was clear to them. Barely a dent had been made in the jar of undyed macaronis, while the jar with the red macaronis was less than half full.

"How come there are fewer red left?" I asked. I gave several children a chance to explain, encouraging the others to listen to their explanations.

"When you made your necklace," I said, "you had to use the red and white macaronis. I didn't give you any choice of colors. Maybe this was okay. Maybe red is your favorite color." Some of the children raised their hands to indicate that this was so.

I continued. "But I bet some of you might like to make a necklace using a different color."

Some of the children started to call out colors they would like to use, but I interrupted them. "Let me explain what your choices are and how I want you to report which color you would like," I said.

I posted the chart paper and wrote on top, "Which color would you choose for your new necklace?" I then set up a bar graph for the children. Using the glue stick, I pasted on the side of the chart one square of each color I had cut and wrote the color name above each square to help the children learn those words. I had chosen colors I knew I could dye the macaronis. I then drew horizontal lines so each color had its own row delineated.

"I want each of you to choose one square of paper," I told the children. "Choose the color that is your favorite, or the one you would like to use to make another necklace. Be thinking about the color you will choose as I pass around the box. When you have your square, write your name on it. Then each of you will come up and paste yours in the correct row." I began to circulate with the squares.

"Do you think everyone will pick the same color?" I asked as children were choosing their colors. I was answered with a chorus of no's.

This was not the first graphing experience the children had had this year, so the children knew how to respond on the graph. It was especially good that this graph was introduced in the context of an activity, with the purpose of gathering information that was needed. It is ideal to have a graph where there is a real purpose for understanding and interpreting the information.

The activity supports children's learning about the usefulness of mathematics for making decisions.

I had the children come up one at a time and paste their squares on the chart with the glue stick. I then talked about the graph.

"Let's count and see how many squares were pasted up," I began. Together the class and I counted twenty-two squares.

"How many children are in the class altogether?" I asked. They knew from their attendance-taking activity each morning that there were twenty-five students.

I then asked, "How many children are absent today?" A few of the children figured it out, but most were not able to do so. Though I had suspected that it would be too difficult for many of the children, asking the question gave me the chance to see who did understand. Also, though most children didn't know how many were absent, many knew who was missing. "Eric's not here." "Nancy's absent." "Richard had to go to the doctor."

I then focused the children on the information posted. "Which color was chosen most often?" I asked. It was clear from the graph that purple was the general favorite. I followed with other questions: "How many children chose purple?" "Which color was the second favorite?" "Which color was chosen

The children come up one at a time and glue their squares on the chart.

least often?" "Which was chosen more—yellow or blue?" "Which color was chosen by three children?"

Then I asked the children to look at the measuring cups I had brought. "Which cup do you think I should use to measure the macaronis we want to dye purple?" "What about yellow?" "What about green?" After all the responses, I asked the children for explanations. Though explaining is difficult for some children, their ease and ability in doing so will increase as they hear others' explanations and have opportunities themselves to verbalize.

I taped colored squares on the cups to mark which to use for each color. I then measured and dyed the macaronis, using food coloring and alcohol, and left them to dry for the next day. Though purple was the favorite color for most of the children, it was hard to get a good color since the yellow of the macaronis makes the purple come out quite brown. The children didn't mind, however, and left knowing that they were going to make necklaces the next day.

MAKING NEW NECKLACES

The next day, children were given the chance to make their new necklaces. They were to use the same pattern they had used before, using dyed macaronis in the sequence of one to six, with white ones in between. I reviewed the directions the children were to follow to make their necklaces.

"Before you make your necklaces," I told the children, "I'd like you to figure out how many macaronis of each color you will need."

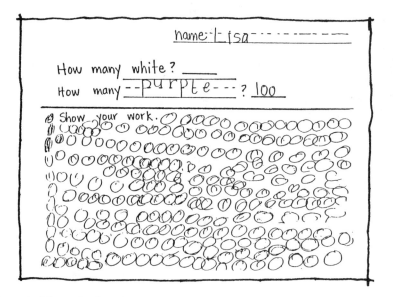

Lisa is not able to deal with the number of purple macaronis she needs.

I showed the children a worksheet I had prepared, on which they were to record how many white and how many dyed macaronis they would use. There was space also for them for figuring out this problem. I was interested in seeing how children would do with this task of solving a numerical problem related to a concrete experience and how they would record their work. As it was early in the school year, the children had not had a great deal of this type of experience.

There was a wide range of responses on the worksheets, both in the solutions and in how children chose to show their work. Some children arrived at correct answers. Others arrived at close answers, just one or two off. Others

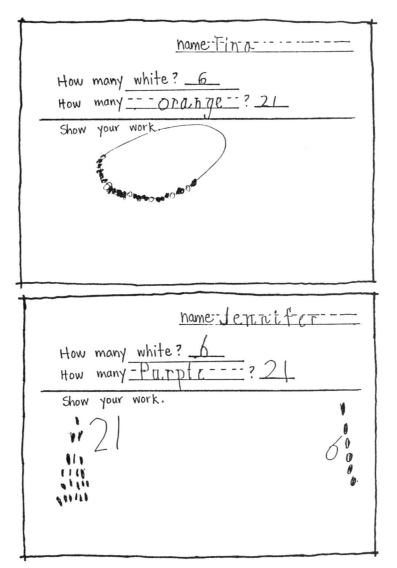

Tina arrives at the answer by drawing a picture of a necklace while Jennifer uses dots in a pattern to represent the macaronis.

recorded answers which seemed to have no discernible relation to the problem at hand. Lisa, for example, thought she'd need 100 purple macaronis, while Michael thought he'd need fifty-two white and fifty-eight orange.

Most children drew pictures to show their work, some showing necklaces, some showing themselves wearing necklaces. The most common approach to the problem was for children to draw the necklace and then count the macaronis they had drawn. One child, Melissa, attempted to solve it by writing an addition problem, but she got confused with how to represent the idea of one more. Jennifer represented the macaronis with dots, arranging them in a pattern that allowed her to find a solution.

From looking at the children's written work, it was obvious to me that recording was too difficult for some of them. However, it was not obvious to the children having the difficulty that it was too difficult. The task engaged the children and gave all of them the opportunity to test their thinking. Also, it provided another piece of information to help me to assess their understanding and to decide about appropriate experiences that might follow.

Melissa tries to solve the problem with addition, but she is confused about how to represent the idea of one more.

Chapter 2
Cows and Chickens and Other Such Problems

This chapter suggests problem situations for young children that present contexts in which to apply mathematical ideas. Problem-solving situations of this kind encourage students to organize and stretch their thinking. Also, they give children experience with using problem-solving strategies.

In these classes, the children worked with partners to solve the problems. For each problem, the children were to agree on a solution and record it. Then the pairs presented to the class what they had done. From discussing problems with partners and presenting their reasoning processes, children gain valuable language experience. In addition, they have the opportunity to hear and learn from others' approaches to thinking.

PRESENTING THE COWS AND CHICKEN PROBLEM TO FIRST GRADERS

"I'm going to tell you a story," I told the class of first graders, thus beginning the lesson. "Listen carefully, because there is a problem for you to think about in this story."

I presented the situation to the children. "I took a ride in the country last weekend and drove past many farms," I told the class. "At one farm, I noticed a farmer standing near the road, looking up at a hill in the distance. He looked very worried. I stopped my car and got out.

" 'Is something wrong?' I asked the farmer.

" 'Yes,' he answered, 'I have a problem that I need to solve. I have one field up on that hill there.' He pointed at the hill. 'There are four cows and three chickens in the field. I know that because I put them there. Also, there is a fence around the field. What I'm wondering is how many feet and tails they have altogether. I'm trying to figure that out without climbing up the hill to the field to count.'

"I told the farmer that I knew a class of children who were learning about solving problems, and I thought the class could figure this out. I'm going to give you a chance to solve the farmer's problem."

I wrote some of the information on the board. This gave me a chance to review the story.

> There are 4 cows.
> There are 3 chickens.
> How many feet and tails are there altogether?

I explained to the children how I wanted them to work. "You won't work alone on this problem," I told the children. "You'll each work with a partner. You and your partner will have one piece of paper for both of you to use together.

"Here is what you and your partner are to do," I continued. "First you need to tell each other what the problem is so that you're sure you both understand it. Then, before starting to write anything on your one piece of paper, you need to talk about what you will put on the paper and how you will share the work."

I then talked about what it was they should be writing. "What you put on the paper should help you solve the problem. It can be a drawing, numbers, or anything that you think will help you. Also, you can use blocks or counters if you'd like."

I paused for questions. There were none, so I continued. "You both must agree on one answer; you can't have two answers for the problem. When you think you have an answer, practice explaining to each other what you did so you can share it with the whole class. When you're both pleased with your solution and your explanations, bring your paper up to the front and sit on the rug."

Because the children were seated in groups of four, it was easy for children to pair up with the children seated next to them. One child, Melissa, had no partner. Melissa was one of the most capable students in the class. I went to her and told her that I thought she would be able to do the problem alone.

"I'll listen to your explanations," I told her.

"Good," Melissa declared, "I know you'll understand what I'm saying."

I reviewed the directions once more before the children began solving the problem, asking students to explain what they were to do first, and next, and so on. The children then went to work.

DURING THE WORK TIME

Just as instructed, the children began by talking about the problem. As I circulated, I marveled at how most of the children plunged into explaining the problem and talking about how they would share the work in a variety of ways. "Each cow has four feet and one tail. Right?" "She said there were four cows and three chickens." "We have to find out how many feet." "Yeah, and how many tails." "You draw the cows, and I'll draw the chickens." "Let's each write our names on the paper first." "Oooh, there are lots of feet." "Let's do tails first."

I noticed that Muhran and Lorene seemed to be having difficulty getting started. "How about starting by telling the story to each other?" I suggested to them. They nodded.

"Who would like to tell the story first?" I asked, and waited. Finally Lorene said she would.

"Okay," I said, "your job, Muhran, is to listen carefully to make sure you agree. Then you take your turn and tell the story to Lorene." I left them to begin.

I had to focus two other pairs of students in the same way. The rest of the students, however, had no trouble getting started. The level of interaction was high. Children were expressing themselves in many different ways and were listening to each other with great intensity.

A typical textbook approach to solving problems lists "Understanding the Problem" as the first step. Having the opportunity to verbalize that understanding can help this process, and I witnessed the benefits of this as the children interacted.

As the pairs worked, making drawings and writing numbers on their papers, I circulated and asked the children questions. I did this to make sure they had dealt with all the information in the problem and to make sure they could explain what particular numbers on their papers meant.

Tina and Mark were wrestling with the problem of agreeing on a number for their solution. They had spread out crayons in a very orderly way on their table to represent the feet and tails. Each had counted the crayons. And though they could easily describe what each crayon represented and were clearly pleased with themselves, they couldn't agree on one answer. Mark thought the answer was 30; Tina thought it was 29.

"What could you do to be sure?" I asked them.

"I'll count the crayons again," Tina offered. This time she counted 28.

After a moment, Mark said in a very determined way, "Let's count them again and push them." They did that together, in a methodical and orderly

Tina and Mark spread out crayons in an orderly way to represent the feet and tails.

way, with Mark pushing each crayon over as it was counted. They were then convinced that 29 was the correct answer.

Other children also used objects to solve the problem. Some worked on their fingers. Many drew pictures of cows and chickens. Some of the drawings were quite elaborate—cows with udders and chickens with beaks and feathers, many with exaggerated tails. A few of the children attempted to write the problem as an addition algorithm.

Melissa, working alone, chose to solve the problem by adding numbers. She explained her figuring to me. First she figured out the cows' feet by adding 4 and 4 and getting 8, then 8 + 4 for another cow, finally 12 + 4 for the fourth cow. Then she wrote 4 + 16 to get 20, which told her how many

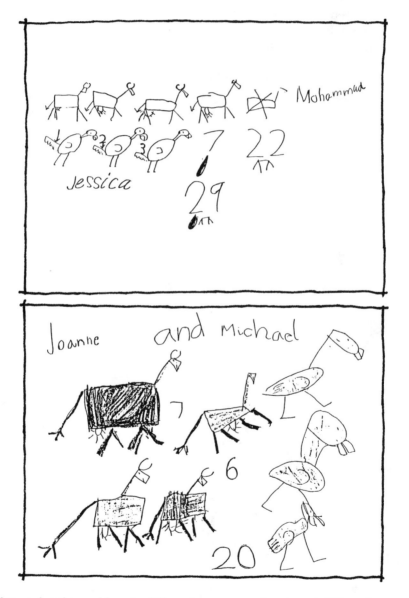

Children solve the problem in different ways—and arrive at different answers.

feet and tails the cows had in all. Then she started on the chickens. She added 3 to the 20 (for the chickens' tails, she explained) and got 23. Then she added on 6 for the chickens' feet, but she did this last computation incorrectly, adding 6 to 20 instead of to the 23. Her final answer was 26, three off. When I questioned her about the error at the end, Melissa was unable, or unwilling, to rethink it. She had had enough.

When most of the children had gathered on the rug, I questioned the others and saw that most of those, too, were just about ready to come up. Michael, however, was reluctant to join the group. His partner, Joanne, had already seated herself on the rug. When I checked with Michael, he said, "But we haven't explained yet. I kept telling Joanne we had to explain, but she just kept on coloring the cows and chickens." I went to the rug and sent Joanne back so they could complete their task.

SUMMARIZING WITH THE CLASS

When everyone was settled on the rug, I asked the children, "How did you like working with a partner?" Expressing their thoughts was difficult for the children.

"I liked it," Nancy said, but when I asked her if she could tell us what she liked about it, she couldn't explain.

Philip said, "Working with a partner makes it faster."

Cynthia said, "You have someone to help you draw."

"I don't like it," Lai said. Then he mumbled, "I like boys better." He was Annie's partner. I asked him if Annie had been helpful as a partner, and Lai begrudgingly nodded yes.

I then asked the children to report the answers they had gotten for the farmer's problem. Their solutions ranged from 20 to 34. Five pairs of children had the correct answer, 29.

Then each pair stood up, showed their papers, and explained what they had done. They did this with varying degrees of ease and efficiency. Mark and Tina, still excited about their crayon layout, both talked at once and could barely get it all out quickly enough. There was a problem hearing the children who spoke very softly, whose hesitancy somehow made it difficult for them to project. Still, the children enjoyed the sharing. Having more of these kinds of opportunities will increase their confidence.

No pair of children asked if their answer was the right one. It seemed that they were all satisfied with their results, even with the discrepancies reported. They did ask, however, if I was taking their papers to the farmer. This seemed much more important to them.

COWS AND CHICKENS IN A SECOND-GRADE CLASS

Later, when I visited a second-grade class to present the same problem, I made two adjustments to the lesson I had done with the first graders. I upped the ante a bit, so the children were asked to figure out how many feet and tails there were for five cows and four chickens. Also, after the children had reported their solutions, I had them write explanations of how they solved this problem. They also worked with partners.

The second graders differed from the first graders in that they were slower to get started. Many were not interested initially in drawing pictures, but came to it when they weren't making headway with just numbers. Several groups of children got counters to use.

In the class discussion, each pair of children showed their papers, and explained what they had done. Children had reached four different solutions—28, 29, 33, and 37. Most had gotten 37, though they had arrived at that answer in different ways.

Danny and Philip presented their solution. They had written 5, 8, 8, 8, 8 in a vertical row and then added them.

"What do those 8s stand for?" I asked.

Neither of the boys could explain, so I gave a prompt. "Do they have to do with a cow and chicken together?" I asked.

Second graders solve the problem of how many feet and tails there are for five cows and four chickens.

That jogged Danny's memory. "Oh, yeah," he said, "for one cow and one chicken, there are eight feet and tails all together. One cow didn't have a partner."

When writing their descriptions, although I hadn't explicitly said they were to write to the farmer, some wrote Dear Farmer letters. Children requested help with spelling words, and I wrote some of the words on the board.

Danny and Philip's writing did not reflect what they had numerically recorded on their paper. They wrote: *"Dear farmer. A cow has 4 legs and 1 tail so that makes 5 each so that makes 25 and a chicken has 2 legs and 1 tail so that makes 37."*

Brian and David were more compassionate than specific. They wrote: *"Dear farmer we are sorry you had this problem. This is how you solve it. 28 + 9 = 37. That is how you solve it. So you can solve it next time. You can draw them and count them."*

From Aaron and Brendon: *"Add the cows legs up 4 by 4 and 5 tails. Add the chicken legs 2 by 2 and 4 tails."*

From Rochelle and Corrine: *"You should count the legs in your mind. Then you should put the numbers on a piece of paper. Then put the tails on the piece of paper and count all of them together."*

From Barbara and Brian: *"Dear farmer Get a paper and draw lines and count them and then add them up."*

From Miho and Tom: "*You get paper and you draw 5 cows and 4 chickens. You count the feet and tails. You add the tails and feet and you get your answer. Your farmers friends.*" They signed their paper.

You get paper and you draw
5 cows and 4 chickens. You
count the feet and tails.
You add the tails and feet
and you get your answer.
Your farmers friends
Miho
Tomo

Miho and Tomo give explicit directions.

Heather and Angie had a long-range view: "*You can get a piece of paper and add the feet and the tails together and count the cows feet and tails and the chickens feets and tails together. Then every other year you count if they have babies.*"

Nema Heather, Angie
You can get a piece of paper and
add the feet and the tails together and
count the cows feet and tails
and the chickens feets and tails together.
Then everyother year you count
if they have babise.
From Heather, Angie

Heather and Angie add a long-range approach to their method for counting feet and tails.

Reem and Stacy offered the farmer two choices: "*You should go to the field and count the feet and the legs or you should count the feet and legs all together.*"

TRICYCLES AND BICYCLES FOR FIRST GRADERS

On another day, I presented a problem to the first graders who had solved the problem about cows and chickens, giving them a second opportunity to work together to solve a problem, to record it in some way, and again to present to their classmates what they had done.

"There was a man who was feeling very proud," I told the children. "He was feeling proud for three reasons. First, he had just invented a special kind of tire that fit any size wheel on bicycles and tricycles. Second, he was proud because he had a factory in which he made these tires."

Brian interrupted the story with a question. "What's a factory?" he asked. I had several children explain what they knew to Brian. "It's a place where they make things." "It's where cars come from." Brian was soon satisfied. I continued with the story.

"A third reason the man was proud was that he had just received his first order. The order said: 'Please send tires for three bicycles and four tricycles.' " I wrote "3 bicycles and 4 tricycles" on the chalkboard.

"Though he was feeling proud," I went on, "he now had a problem to solve. How many tires should he send?"

I told the children that I would like them to try to solve this problem. I talked with them about how many wheels there were on bicycles and tricycles to make sure they all knew.

As with the problem about cows and chickens, I organized them into pairs. I told the children that they were to tell each other the story to make sure they both understood it, then together to find a solution and record it on one piece of paper, and finally to practice explaining their solution to be ready to explain it to the class.

All but two pairs of the children arrived at the correct solution of eighteen tires. However, pairs of children worked in different ways.

Nancy and Jennifer used counters, organizing them into groups of three for the tricycles and groups of two for the bicycles. They counted them to get their answer. Then they drew pictures of the counters on their paper and wrote "18" to show their solution.

Mohammad and Jessica divided the task. Mohammad worked on the bicycles, carefully drawing them. He got so involved that he drew four of them, but then crossed out one. Jessica drew only the wheels for the tricycles, putting them in four neat boxes. They then counted twelve wheels for the tricycles and six wheels for bicycles. Jessica wrote 6 + 12. She then called me over and said, "I can't do 12 and 6." But then she jumped up and got Unifix cubes, and she and Mohammad worked together, using red cubes for bicycle wheels and white cubes for tricycle wheels.

Tina and Mark used a different system of teamwork. Mark drew the bicycles and tricycles, and Tina filled in the spokes on the wheels. After they counted the tires together, Tina wrote "18" in the center of the paper.

Philip and Yovan solved the problem by drawing just wheels on their paper.

The two pairs who didn't find the correct answer drew all the needed bicycles and tricycles. Lisa and Derek had gotten so involved coloring their drawings, even including a road with a dotted line down the center, that they seemed to have no energy left for the numbers. Randy and Annie wrote "4 + 3 = 7" as their solution.

MORE PROBLEMS

In the following weeks, I presented other problem-solving experiences of this type to the same first graders. I used the same format for organization in the classroom. For each situation, I told the children the story, then organized them into partners to work, and finally called the class together for the children to share their solutions. With each experience, the children's abilities to work together, find solutions, and present explanations improved.

During the time when the class was studying about various animals, I introduced the following problem: "Four raccoons went down to the lake for a drink," I said. "Two got their front feet wet. One got its back feet wet. How many dry feet were there?"

Another day, I presented this situation: "Some children went out to play in the snow. When they came in, they put their boots by the door to dry. There were twelve boots. How many children put their boots by the door?"

When the class was learning about eating with chopsticks, I presented the children with another problem: "Suppose we were going to have Chinese food and I was going to bring chopsticks for everyone to use. How many chopsticks would I need to bring?" Getting started on this problem required that we figure out how many children there were altogether. We talked about ways to do this, finally counting off to get to 27. "Will you be eating with us?" Rachel wanted to know. "Yes," I said, and the children got to work.

COUNTING FEET

Leslie Salkeld teaches pre-first graders in Edison, Washington. Her students are drawn from the entire district. They have completed kindergarten, but aren't quite ready for a standard first grade. In Leslie's class, they have an extra year to mature and have additional experiences to prepare them better for first grade.

Leslie had read the description of the problem about the feet and tails of cows and chickens and wanted to do a similar problem with her students. However, she wanted to present a situation that related more closely to her students' direct experiences.

To do this, Leslie presented a problem to a group of six children she had gathered around a table during reading time. "How many feet do you think there are under the table right now?" she asked. "Don't peek just yet. Let's see how we could figure that out together."

Marc volunteered that there were twelve. "I just counted everyone's eyes," he explained, "because we have the same number of eyes as feet."

Other children had different ideas for figuring out the problem, and the group tried each of the suggestions. They went around the group and counted by ones, with each child saying two numbers in succession. They counted by twos together. Each child took two blocks, and the group counted them altogether. Finally, they looked underneath the table to find out for sure.

After repeating this experience with the other reading groups over the next few days, Leslie introduced a class graph during math time. She had the children record how many people lived in their houses, counting themselves

The children are figuring out how many feet are under the table.

as well. Using the information reported on the graph, Leslie organized the children into groups, putting together those who had the same number living in their houses.

The problem for each group was to figure out how many feet would be under the table if everyone in their family ate together. Groups reported their results, and one child from each group colored in that group's answer on a 0–99 chart Leslie had posted.

A few days later, Leslie extended the activity further. To review what they had done so far, she called the children's attention to the 0–99 chart and asked who could explain what the numbers that were colored in told. Several children offered explanations.

"Three people live in my house," Leslie said, "my husband; my son, Craig; and me. What number would I color in?" It was not difficult for the children to discuss this and come up with the answer 6.

Then Leslie introduced a new idea. "Coloring in the number 6 doesn't tell the whole story of who lives in my house," she said. "We also have a cat and a dog."

Leslie demonstrated several different ways she could figure out how many feet there are altogether in her house, including those of her pets. She drew pictures on the board and had the children count the feet with her. She used Unifix cubes, making trains of two for her, Mr. Salkeld, and Craig, and trains of four for the cat and dog. She figured aloud for the children, "Four and four are eight, and that takes care of the cat and the dog. Then I have to add two for me, my husband, and my son. So that's eight plus two are ten, plus two are twelve, plus two more are fourteen." Leslie colored in the number 14 on the 0–99 chart.

Leslie then gave the children an assignment. "You are to figure out how many feet there are in your house altogether," she said. "Record your answer and how you found it." The children went to work and continued working on the problem the next day.

The mathematical potential of the problem continued to grow. When they had all finished, the children reported how they had solved the problem, then they colored their answers on the 0–99 chart. One child colored in the number 11, and that was the only number that was not in a column of even numbers. It provided the opportunity for a discussion about odd and even numbers.

Some children arrived at the same number, but for different reasons. For example, one child also reported 14, as did Leslie, but there were four people, one parakeet, and one dog in his house. This led to another kind of problem—who could be living in a house for any of the numbers colored in?

The work on feet continued for quite a while.

Chapter 3
Riddles with Color Tiles

These lessons emphasize logical reasoning and language skills while helping to develop children's number sense. Building on children's interest in riddles, the lessons present students with clues to decipher in order to determine which Color Tiles were put into a bag. The Color Tiles are one-inch-square tiles in four colors—red, blue, yellow, and green.

The children analyze each of the clues and then display with their tiles what they know. Each successive clue narrows the possibilities, until there is sufficient information to declare what is in the bag. The children later create their own riddles for others to solve.

INTRODUCING THE FIRST RIDDLE

Because the children had not yet explored with the Color Tiles, I began by giving them a chance to do so. I've learned from experience that if children's curiosity about a material is not satisfied, they will not focus on the lesson being presented. Time for their own exploration is essential.

The amount of time children need for this free exploration differs from class to class. Also, the nature of the material is a factor. In this instance, I gave the children fifteen minutes before asking for their attention. I told them I wanted them to try an activity I had planned with the Color Tiles. I judged from their responses that most were willing to stop their own exploring. However, if they were so involved that they couldn't refocus, I would have allowed more time.

Once I had their attention, I asked, "What is a riddle?" The children had various thoughts about that. "It's something you have to guess." "You get clues." "Sometimes it's funny." "Sometimes they rhyme."

"I have a riddle about what's in this bag," I told the class. I had put four blue tiles and two yellow tiles into a lunch bag.

"My riddle has clues," I continued, "and I will tell you the clues one at a time. After each clue, I'll ask you to think about what I could have in the bag. Then you and your partner will talk about what information you have about the tiles in my bag and use your tiles to show what you know."

I then gave the class the first clue. "I have fewer than ten tiles," I said, and wrote that on the chalkboard. "What could I have in the sack?"

Russell raised his hand. "Could it be ten tiles?" he asked. This gave me the opportunity to clarify what "fewer than" means.

The children talked with their partners and displayed possibilities with their tiles. I had them describe what the tiles showed and what they knew. There were various responses.

Neil explained for himself and Stacy why they thought there were nine tiles. "We put out ten tiles," he said, "and then took away one, so we think there are nine."

Ari and Samuel had carefully laid out nine lines of tiles, with nine, eight, seven, and so on, down to a line with only one tile. "It could be nine or eight or seven or six or five or four or three or two or one," Ari explained.

None of the others were so organized. Most displayed either a few possibilities, or showed just one prediction, as did Neil and Stacy. Elissa and Jason, for example, placed six tiles in a line. Elissa reported, "We think there are six tiles." When I asked why they had decided on six, however, neither of them could supply a reason.

The different responses from the children did not surprise or disturb me. I knew they would have a chance to reconsider with later clues.

I then presented the second clue. "There are two colors," I said, writing this clue under the first one. "Talk about this with your partner and show with your tiles what you think I could have put into the bag."

Again, the children discussed and reported what they thought. Some kept what they had had before, making adjustments so they had two colors. Some changed completely what they had. Molly and Jenny displayed just two tiles, one red and one yellow. They ignored the previous information about how many tiles, and merely focused on the colors.

I then gave my third clue and wrote it on the chalkboard. "I have no green or red tiles," I said. The children scurried to make changes on their desks.

"What do you now know for sure?" I asked. Many hands went up.

I called on Rodney. "You only used blue and yellow," he said.

"What else do you know for sure?" I asked.

Fewer hands were raised. "There are less than ten tiles," Jennifer responded.

"What else do you know for sure?" I continued.

"You could have six tiles," Sharon said.

"I might," I said, "but you can't say how many tiles I have for sure yet. I'll give you another clue that will help you begin to figure out how many I have in the bag."

I then gave the fourth clue. "I have twice as many blue tiles as yellow tiles," I said. After writing that clue on the board, I asked, "Who knows what I mean by 'twice as many'?"

Only two of the children in the class responded that they knew. Though both could show what they thought with their tiles, neither could verbalize what "twice as many" meant. Children need a great deal of experience in explaining to develop language appropriate for describing their thoughts.

I explained the concept of "twice" to the children by using other words— double, two times, that many again—and the color tiles. "Put out three red tiles and three blue tiles," I directed the children. "Now put out another three blue tiles. That gives you twice as many blue tiles. How many blue tiles do you have?" When they answer, I can say that six is twice as many as three. "It's double the amount." I did several other examples such as this one with the children.

There were murmurs of recognition. Children seemed to remember knowing about the idea of "twice."

I went on to my fifth clue. "I have two yellow tiles in the bag," I said, and added this clue to the list already on the board. "Now discuss with your partner what could possibly be in the sack."

Ari was eager to report his discovery. He was sure that there were two yellow tiles and four blue tiles in the bag and explained how he had figured it out. "I put two yellow and two blue down, and then I put two more blue," he said.

"That's what I think too," Darwin said. Several others nodded in agreement.

"So you're willing to guess what's in the bag?" I asked Ari. He nodded confidently.

"Is anyone else willing to guess what's in the bag?" I asked the class. Only a few raised their hands.

"I think I know," Elizabeth said, a bit tentatively.

"Do we get another clue?" Jason asked.

'What about Ari's idea?" I asked.

"I think we need another clue," Darwin said. Though he agreed with Ari, he still felt the need for a further check.

"I have six tiles," I said, writing this sixth clue on the chalkboard. That resolved it for the class. They watched eagerly as I emptied the bag and showed them the four blue tiles and the two yellow tiles.

The sixth clue resolves the riddle for the children.

THE CHILDREN WRITE RIDDLES

I gave the children directions for writing their own riddles. "You and your partner will write a riddle together for others to solve," I explained. "For your riddle, use no more than ten tiles and only two colors."

I then outlined the procedure. "I'll give you and your partner one piece of paper, a lunch bag, and a clothespin. First you decide together what to put into the sack. Then write clues so others can guess. Finally, attach your clues to the bag with a clothespin and put the bag on top of the bookcase. You can begin now and work until it's time for recess. You can continue working on your riddle tomorrow."

The children had difficulty with this assignment. Most began by focusing on the colors they had chosen, giving clues for these. *"The colors are dark." "The colors start with a b and a y." "The colors are not red or yellow." "The colors are kind of bright." "The colors are in the room." "There are some green."*

After this, however, most groups got into difficulty. "What do we do now?" was a common question asked of me. I let them work, however, as I think there is benefit in struggling a bit as long as the frustration doesn't become overwhelming and cloud the children's interest in the activity. Also, watching the children work helps me learn more about individual thinking processes and problem-solving abilities.

The next day, after all had done some work on their riddles, I called the children together. I told them that I knew that all their riddles weren't finished yet, but that I wanted to talk about what they had done. "I'm going to have some of you read your clues to the class," I said. "Together we'll decide if you have enough clues or if you still need more."

We did this for several of the children's riddles, and it seemed to help them focus on the need to test their clues to see if they were sufficient. Still, it was clear to me that further experience was needed, and I planned to do another riddle with the class the next day.

A SECOND RIDDLE

The children were excited the next day when I told them I had another tile riddle for them to solve. I reminded them that after each clue, they were to talk to each other, decide together what could be in the bag, and use tiles to show what they thought were possibilities.

I gave the first clue. "There are twelve tiles," I said, and wrote that clue on the chalkboard. The children immediately began talking and counting out tiles. They seemed much more comfortable this time. "I think it's all yellow." "I think it's six blue and six red." "It could be four colors and three of each."

Some pairs of children placed twelve tiles in a line. Others arranged theirs in an array. Some displayed just one possibility, while others showed several possibilities.

Before presenting the next clue to the children, I asked them to share their thoughts. "One from each pair is to tell what you have in front of you," I explained, "while the rest of the class listens."

After this reporting, I gave the second clue. "I used three colors," I said, writing this clue under the first one. Again, the children got busy arranging tiles and talking. Most made changes in what they had shown so their possibilities had three colors.

Ari and Samuel tried to figure out how many different ways they could have three colors, filling their table with arrays of tiles. Others still held to a single prediction. Molly and Jenny, for example, showed one line of twelve tiles with five blue, five red, and two yellow. Russell and Miles made the same prediction, but arranged their tiles into an array with a row of five green, a row of five blue, and a row of two yellow.

Getting the children to stop work and refocus on a discussion was more difficult this time. Some were eager to continue exploring possibilities. Others had begun to play and build with the tiles. Even after several reminders, many were distracted by the tiles when they were supposed to be listening to each other.

I instituted a system for bringing them to attention so they wouldn't continue to fiddle with the tiles during our discussions. "From now on," I said, "when I put a star on the chalkboard, that means no one can touch the tiles. I think it is important for you to listen to each other, and I think not touching the tiles will help. After we spend a little time talking, I will erase the star, and then you can go back to work with the tiles." I drew a star on the board, and all of the children took their hands off their desktops. This system turned out to be a tremendous help.

After they reported their conclusions from the second clue, I gave the third. "I have no red tiles," I said. I wrote this clue on the chalkboard and then erased the star.

The children got busily involved making changes in the possibilities they had displayed, reminding each other that it had to be three colors and that there had to be twelve tiles. Most just eliminated the red tiles, replacing them with other colors. Russell and Miles were even more convinced that their prediction of five green, five blue, and two yellow was correct.

When I wanted to refocus them for a discussion, I walked to the chalkboard and drew a star. This time, it took little effort to get their attention.

Before having them share their thinking, I told them what I was able to observe as I watched them work. "I could tell many things from looking at what was on your desks," I said. "I could tell who was working together. I could tell if you were using all the clues on the chalkboard. I could tell what your ideas were." Then I had children share what they now thought might be in the bag.

I continued with the fourth clue. "There are the same number of blue tiles as green tiles," I said. I wrote this clue on the chalkboard. The children looked at me patiently.

"You didn't erase the star," Elissa pointed out.

I erased it, and the children got to work.

This clue helped some of the children more accurately define the possibilities. Once again, the number of possibilities they placed in front of them varied. A few pairs found all five possibilities; some found two or three; a few still showed only one choice.

I drew a star on the chalkboard and called them back to attention. This time I recorded their predictions as they reported them.

$$6y + 3b + 3g$$
$$2y + 5b + 5g$$
$$8y + 2b + 2g$$
$$4y + 4b + 4g$$
$$10y + 1b + 1g$$

"Are there any more possibilities?" I asked.

Ari raised his hand. "You can't have six blue and six green because that would be twelve already, and you wouldn't have any yellow," he said.

No one could think of other possibilities.

Then I put a loop around the column that listed the yellow tiles and asked what they noticed about what I had circled.

$$6y + 3b + 3g$$
$$2y + 5b + 5g$$
$$8y + 2b + 2g$$
$$4y + 4b + 4g$$
$$10y + 1b + 1g$$

"They all are yellow," Mary said.

"They all are counting by twos," Samuel said.

No one had any other comments. "What can you say about the numbers that tell how many blue and green tiles could be in the bag?" I asked.

"Those are just counting by ones," Miles said.

I then gave the class the fifth clue. "I have four yellow tiles," I said, and added this one to the list of clues. This last clue told the rest of the story for all the children. After a few minutes, each pair had a single tile arrangement showing four yellow, four blue, and four green tiles. There were no doubts, and no one needed an additional clue.

A SECOND CHANCE AT WRITING RIDDLES

"I'd like you to get back to writing your own riddles again," I said. "You can continue working on the riddle you started, or you can begin again and count that one as practice."

This time, the assignment was greeted with much enthusiasm. Again, I presented them with the same guidelines. "Remember, you are to use no more than ten tiles and only two colors. First, agree on the tiles to put into the bag, and then write clues so others can figure it out. Call me over to check your riddle when you've finished it." There was none of the confusion this time as the children began work on their riddles.

The children continued working on their riddles during math time the next day. To engage those who finished writing their riddles more quickly, I had prepared two sets of clues. This way, children who completed their own

Jason and Elissa work together to write their own riddle.

riddles had new problems to consider while those who needed more time to work could have it. I wrote each set of clues on large chart paper, clipping the matching bag of tiles to it.

Extra Riddle No. 1

Clue No. 1: There are ten tiles in the bag.
Clue No. 2: There are three colors.
Clue No. 3: There are three blue tiles.
Clue No. 4: There are two more red tiles than blue tiles.
Clue No. 5: There are three more red tiles than yellow tiles.

Extra Riddle No. 2

Clue No. 1: There are more than six tiles in the bag.
Clue No. 2: There are three colors.
Clue No. 3: There are four green tiles.
Clue No. 4: There are half as many yellow tiles as green tiles.
Clue No. 5: There is one more blue tile than green tiles.

Having the extra riddles made me available to provide help to children who needed it. Russell and Miles, for example, had written a riddle with six clues. Their clues were:

1. *We have more yellows then the other colore.*
2. *One is the colore of the sun.*
3. *One is the colore of the sea.*
4. *And it is dark.*
5. *The colores are around the room.*
6. *I bet you can't ges how many blues and yellows there are.*

Russell and Miles were right. I couldn't guess how many blues and yellows were in the bag from those six clues. I talked with them about also needing clues that gave me information about how many tiles there were, not just about their colors. I directed the boys to look at the clues I had written that gave hints about how many tiles were in the bag. I left them to work, and they added two additional clues:

7. *There are 2 more yellow than blue.*
8. *There are 10 all together.*

After Russell and Miles add the seventh and eighth clues, their riddle is complete.

Stacy and Neil's riddle provides sufficient clues for guessing how many tiles of each color are in the bag.

Stacy + Neil
1. We have no yellows.
2. We have 1 red.
3. There are more blues then red.
4. There is more then 2.
5. We have no greens.
6. We have more then 7.
7. We have 8 more blues then red.

I encountered the same situation with Jason and Elissa and handled it in a similar manner. The five clues they had written were not sufficient. They were pleased with the sixth clue they added to their final version. They wrote:

> 1. There are ten.
> 2. There are six of one color.
> 3. We have some reds.
> 4. There are no yellow.
> 5. There are no green.
> 6. There are less blues.

Stacy and Neil wrote a sufficient set of clues without prompting:

> 1. We have no yellows.
> 2. We have 1 red.
> 3. There are more blues then red.
> 4. There is more then 2.
> 5. We have no greens.
> 6. We have more then 7.
> 7. We have 8 more blues then red.

When the children had completed their riddles, they took turns presenting them to the class. One or two pairs of children presented their clues each day until the class had deciphered all of the riddles.

Jason Lee
Jennifer Tsoo
                    Riddles

1 There are ten tiles,

2 There are two colers.

3 The colers are kind of light.

4 There are no green and red.

5 There are more yellow than blue.

6 There are four blue,

Jason and Jennifer add the fourth clue to clarify the colors.

Chapter 4
Estimating Beans

Third graders are involved with estimation in this lesson. The children estimate how many scoops of beans are needed to fill a jar and organize their estimates into a class graph. Five scoops are then put into the jar, and the children are given the opportunity to revise their estimates.

After finding out how many scoops it takes to fill the jar, children focus on figuring out how many beans the jar holds. Each group counts a scoopful and reports the results. The children then analyze these samples to estimate the total number of beans.

Children get experience with a variety of math concepts in the context of estimating beans. They interpret graphical information, make an intuitive judgment about average, solve a multiplication problem using repeated addition, and use larger numbers.

ESTIMATING SCOOPS OF BEANS

To prepare for the lesson, I collected several materials—a jar, a coffee scoop, enough red kidney beans to fill the jar, and a pad of postnotes. I showed these materials to the children. They were especially fascinated with the postnotes and eager to learn what they were going to do with them.

"I'd like each of you to make an estimate," I said, "about how many scoops of beans you think it will take to fill this jar. You'll write your estimate on a postnote. Then we'll use your postnotes to create a graph of your estimates on the chalkboard." The children had had experiences with estimating before this lesson. They used the word *estimate* interchangeably with the word *guess* and were comfortable with the idea.

While the children were deciding on their estimates, I numbered across the chalkboard from 1 to 26, stopping when I had almost reached the end of the board. I spaced the numbers so postnotes would fit below them.

"Did anyone estimate that it would take one scoop to fill the jar?" I asked, pointing to the l on the board. I had no takers. "Two?" I asked. Still no takers. "Three, four, five, six, seven?" Jill raised her hand for seven, so I stopped and had her come up and place her postnote under the 7 on the chalkboard. She was the only child who had made an estimate of seven, so I continued counting, having children come and place their postnotes when I called the estimate they had made.

When all of the children had posted their estimates, I called their attention to the graph. "What is the smallest guess?" I asked. They answered that it was seven, Jill's estimate.

"What is the largest?" I asked, and they responded with twenty-five.

"Listen to what I say," I continued. "The range of estimates on our graph is from seven to twenty-five. Who can explain what I mean by that?" Several children volunteered. I called on Teddy.

"It means that the guesses go from seven up to twenty-five," he explained. There were nods of agreement.

Erika had another way to explain this. "It means that the smallest guess is seven and the biggest is twenty-five, and there are guesses in between," she said. The others nodded again. No one else volunteered to respond.

"Which number was chosen the most?" I then asked, and the children identified that it was eleven.

"There is a word that describes what occurs most on a graph," I explained. "It's called the mode." I wrote the word *mode* on the chalkboard, and I also wrote the other words I had been using—*graph, estimate, guess,* and *range.* Introducing appropriate vocabulary is best done in the context of an experience, and this was a ripe opportunity for doing so.

"Now that we have your estimates, how could we find out how many scoops are needed to fill the jar?" I asked.

"Do it!" several children responded in unison.

I began to fill the jar with scoops of beans. I stopped after five scoops. The jar was now slightly less than half full.

"Seeing how full the jar is with five scoops gives you information you didn't have when you made your estimate," I said to the class. "Would any of you like to change your mind now about your first estimate?" Most of the children raised their hands.

"First discuss what you think with the others in your group," I directed the children. "Then I'll give any of you who would like the chance to move your postnote to a new estimate."

It is important to me to encourage children to be willing to express their thinking. I realize that doing so requires them to take risks at times. An estimate, for example, could be wrong, even very far off. I want to establish the understanding in the class that a wrong answer is not such a terrible thing. For that reason, I often tell children that it is okay to change their minds, that learning often requires thinking about something in a new way. The postnotes help give concrete support to this philosophy.

Almost all of the children opted to move their postnotes. It was interesting to me that children did not always make the same decisions as other group members. And that was fine, as I had not asked them to come to a group consensus about an estimate.

After all of the children who wanted to had moved their estimates, the guesses ranged from nine to seventeen. Alana, however, had asked me to add more numbers to the chalkboard so she could place her postnote under the number 29.

"If you don't use full scoops of beans," she explained, "you could maybe squeeze in twenty-nine." Even after I assured her that I was going to use full scoops, she chose to let her estimate stand.

"What is the mode of this graph?" I asked the class.

"Twelve," the children responded together.

"Who can explain why twelve is the mode?" I asked.

Though there is a bit of room left, the twelfth scoop of beans spills over.

Gabe explained, "Because twelve was guessed the most." Others nodded in agreement.

I then finished filling the jar. The jar held eleven scoops, and though there was still a bit of room, the twelfth scoop spilled over.

FIGURING THE TOTAL NUMBER OF BEANS.

"We now know that the jar holds about eleven scoops of beans," I said. "But this information doesn't tell how many beans are in the jar. Does anyone have an idea about how we could find out how many beans there are?" I gave the children a few moments to think about this question and then had them offer their suggestions.

Chris said, "If you knew how many beans were in one scoop, then you could add that eleven times."

Others agreed, but Jill had a concern. "The beans aren't all the same size, so you couldn't be sure how many are in a scoop. I think we should pass some beans out to each student and then we could each count some and then add them up."

Tiare had another idea. "Just dump them out and count them," she said.

Patrick offered a refinement. "You could dump them out and then count them by twos," he said, "and it would go faster."

Marina, Kendra, and Bryce use the range of samples reported to decide on an estimate of how many beans fill one scoop.

I then suggested that we try Chris's idea. The class was agreeable. "To find out how many beans there are in a scoop," I said, "I'll give each group a scoop of beans to count. First, decide as a group how you'll count them. Then do it. After you've counted, I'll ask each group to report how many beans you have, and how you went about finding out. I'll record each group's results on the board. Then we can see about Jill's idea that scoops will have different numbers of beans in them."

I gave a scoop to each of the seven groups and gave them time to count. Groups reported different ways of counting.

Chris, Brandie, Tiare, and Bayard made groups of fives. They counted fifty-four beans, ten groups of five with four left over.

Teddy, Grace, Laura, and Jill shared the beans. They passed them out one by one, and each had fourteen beans. Then they added in their heads— 14 + 14 are 28, and 28 + 28 are 56.

Erika, Tara, and Andreas also shared their beans. Each had sixteen, and there were two left over. They reported fifty altogether.

Bryce, Marina, and Kendra didn't worry about sharing the beans equally; each just took a pile and counted them. Marina wrote the numbers they reported on a piece of paper and added them.

I recorded the results from all seven groups on the board as they reported them: 54, 56, 51, 58, 61, 54, 50.

"Two groups get 54," Patrick commented, "but all the other numbers are different."

"That's pretty much what Jill said would happen," Mairead added.

I then gave the class two problems to work on in their groups. The first problem provided an intuitive experience with the concept of average; the second gave them experience using information to estimate the total number of beans.

"First, I want you to decide what one number would be reasonable to use for how many beans fill a scoop," I told the children. "Then use that number to figure out about how many beans the jar can hold."

Marina, Kendra, and Bryce used the range of the numbers of beans in the scoops and wrote: "*We think that is about 55. We think this because 55 is inbertween 50 and 61. We think that there is 605 beans in the jar. We think this because we added 11 55s and it came out 605.*"

Though it was Chris's suggestion originally to add the beans in eleven scoops, his group added their seven counts instead. Bayard, Chris, Tiare, and Brandie wrote: "*We think that fifty four, because we counted how many beans where in the cup, so thats why we think that is the answer. We think there are 384. We added.*"

From Shaney, Nick, Mairead, and Gabe: "*We think there is about 50 beans in a scoop. Because we got 60 beans in are scoop. We got too much. We think there is about 550 beans in the jar because it sounds right.*"

Michelle, Tim, Michael, and Alana wrote: "*We think there are about 56 beans in one scoop. We think there are about 616 beans in one jar. We figured this out by adding 56 11 times and we came up with 616 beans in one jar.*"

Though it was time for recess, Grace chose to remain behind. She was interested in figuring out how many beans there were in the seven scoops the groups had reported, and wrote about how she figured this out: "*I wanted to find out how many beans the class had in all. I looked at all the answers. I decided I might not get the right answer but I would try to add them. I added 4 + 6 and got 10. I added 8 + 1 + 1 + 10 and got 20. Then I added 4. I wrote 4 in my mind so I would not forget the second number. I added four 5s and then added the 2 onto the 20 from the four fives. I added 6 to 22 and I got 28. Then I added the two fives and got ten. I added one more ten and my total was 384 beans in all.*" With a sigh of pleasure, she gave me her paper and said, "I love to write."

A FURTHER NOTE

For a similar lesson in estimating beans, taught to second graders who were learning about place value, read Chapter 6: Making Tens and Ones.

Shaney
Nick
Mairead
~~Gabe~~

We think there is about 50 beans in a scoop. Because we got 60 beans in are scoop. We got too much. We think there is about 550 beans in the jar because it sounds right.

Shaney, Nick, Mairead, and Gabe are not able to explain clearly how they arrive at their answer.

Chapter 5
Sharing Problems

These lessons with third graders help build children's number sense and develop understanding of the process of division. Division isn't generally on the teaching agenda for the beginning of the third grade. These problem-solving activities, however, do not focus on teaching algorithmic procedures for division. Instead, they provide experience with the concept, process, and symbolism of division.

The four lessons described were taught from early October to mid-December. Thus, children had the opportunity to build understanding over time with the chance to return to ideas several times. Further experiences continued throughout the year.

INTRODUCING THE FIRST LESSON

"Four children were walking to school," I told the class. "On the way, they found a five-dollar bill. When they got to school, they told their teacher. She said that the principal would probably be the person who would find out who lost it. The children told the principal and gave her the five-dollar bill.

"A week later, however, the principal called the four children into her office and told them no one had claimed the money. 'It's yours,' she said, 'but you'll have to share it equally among the four of you.' "

After telling the story, I gave the children the problem to solve. "Your job is to figure out how much each child would get," I said. "Work together as a group and record your answer on one sheet of paper."

I showed them on the chalkboard what I wanted them to write. "You need to put each of your names on the paper," I explained. "Work together to figure out the answer. When you've figured it out, you need to write on your group paper, 'Each person gets _____,' and fill in the blank. Also write, 'We think this because' and explain your reasoning." This was a beginning writing assignment in math for the class, and I believed the structure for organizing their thoughts would be helpful.

All of the groups were able to figure out that each child got $1.25. The children's ease with the problem came from their familiarity with money; they knew there were four quarters in one dollar. Figuring the mathematics was less problematic for them than working together and recording.

Since it was early in the school year, the children were still learning how to discuss their thoughts, how to listen to one another, how to negotiate when choosing a recorder, and how to collaborate to produce one written response. These skills take time to develop. With prompting and prodding, all groups completed the assignment.

Tiare recorded for Chris, Brandie, Bayard, and herself. *"Each person gets a dollar twenty-five. We think this because we had a $5 bill and we slipt it so each child got a dollar so then we thought of quaters and that is how we got our answer."* Also, Bayard showed on another piece of paper how the shares could be figured by giving each person five quarters; then he added to show that each would have $1.25.

From Michelle, Michael, Timothy, and Alana: *"Each person gets $1.25. We think this because if each person got a dollar there would be one dollar left. And there are four quarters in a dollar. So everybody gets a $1.25."*

Erika, Ann, Andreas, and Jason described how they would go about disbursing the money in their solution: *"They went to the store and traded for some qurters. So they each get $1.25 because thats equal. We would be more intrested in a more difecolt problom."*

Done By   Chris
          Brandie
          Tiare
          Bayard

Each person gets a dollar twenty-five. We think this because we had a $5,bill and we slipt it so each child got a dollar so then we thought of quaters and that is how we got our anwser.

Erika | Andreas
Ann | Jason

They went to the store and traded for some qurters. So they each get $1.25 because thats equal. We would be more intrested in a more difecolt problom.

To divide $1.25 among four children, both of these groups make a concrete reference to quarters in their solution.

Sharing fifty cents among four children poses a problem with a remainder.

> Michelle   Timothy
> Michael   Alana!!!
>
> We think each person gets 12¢
> and there would be 2¢ left over
> that they could not split up, but
> they could buy bubble-gum with
> the two cents and split the gum.
> We think this because we have
> to share the last two cents.

I gave another problem to the groups who finished first. "What if the children had found fifty cents instead of a five-dollar bill? How would they share that amount?" I asked. This was more difficult for the children because the solution wasn't as visual, and, when divided equally, there would be money remaining. Still, the three groups who tried it solved it correctly.

Michelle, Michael, Timothy, and Alana reported the following: *"We think each person gets 12¢ and there would be 2¢ left over that they could not split up, but they could buy bubble-gum with the two cents and split the gum. We think this because we have to share the last two cents."*

From Erika, Ann, Andreas, and Jason: *"Each person would get 12¢ on the way to the store Andreas skraped his knee whith the extra 2¢ we bougt Andreas a bandaid."*

After the children had reported their findings, I introduced them to the mathematical way to record what they had described in words. "Mathematicians often use symbols to write what they are thinking. Let me show you."

I wrote on the chalkboard: $\$5.00 \div 4 = \$1.25$. I told them that this was a shortcut way to describe the story I had told them earlier. I repeated the story, referring to what I had written. Then I told the class that I had given some of the groups another problem to do. "I'll write the problem I gave them with mathematical symbols," I told the children and wrote on the board: 50¢ ÷ 4.

"Let's see if someone who has not heard the problem can tell the story from what I wrote on the board," I said. "Those of you who know what the problem is, listen and see if you agree with the story being told." Several children were able to interpret the symbols. Then I showed how I would record the answers the children got, introducing the use of "R" for the remainder: 50¢ ÷ 4 = 12¢ R 2¢.

This lesson in sharing gave the children a problem-solving experience with division and also introduced them to linking the appropriate symbolism to the process.

THE SECOND LESSON

In the next lesson, I wanted to build on the "Sharing the Five-dollar Bill" problem. I prepared for the lesson by snapping together a train of seventeen Unifix cubes for each group. I propped the trains vertically on a desktop so the children could see that all the trains were the same length. "How many cubes do you think there are in each of these trains?" I asked. Most of the children volunteered to answer. Their estimates ranged from ten to twenty-one.

I then gave the children the following directions: "I'm going to give each group one of these trains. Your job is to divide the cubes into four equal shares." Two of the groups had only three children in them, but I wanted them all to solve the same problem, so I added to the directions. "Even if there are only three people in your group, you are to divide the cubes into four equal groups. After you've done that, I'll ask each group to report how many each person got and how you did it."

For this experience, I did not ask that they do any recording. I was more interested in keeping their focus on solving the problem concretely. Also, since writing was difficult for some when they shared the five-dollar bill, I thought that focusing on their verbalization without having to write would be helpful.

I realized that further directions were necessary as soon as I gave one of the trains to the nearest group. Four pairs of hands immediately reached for the cubes, breaking the train into several pieces. Before handing out any more cubes, I called the children back to attention.

"I need to tell you one more thing before you get started," I said. "Your first job is to discuss the problem in your group and come up with a plan for sharing the cubes. Once you have a plan, then you can divide the cubes. So no one should touch the cubes at all until you all agree on your plan for solving the problem."

In order to make sure the directions were clear, I asked, "Who can describe what your group's task is?" I had several children give the directions in their own words. They then got to work.

It took the groups about fifteen minutes to divide the cubes. The children worked well together, and were interested in the problem. When they were done, they reported the different ways they had accomplished the task.

Shaney reported for her group. "We just gave one cube to each person," she said, "and kept going around and around until they were all used up. We each have four cubes, and there is one extra."

Teddy explained next. "We did it like that, but we passed them out by twos. We each got four cubes, too."

"We did it like that too, sort of," Erika explained, "but we just passed the whole train around and each person took one until they were all gone. I went first. But then I had one more, so I had to put that in the center of the table."

Patrick's group did it differently. "We divided the train in half, but one half was longer, so we took off one cube. Then we divided each half again. We

These children solve the problem by passing the train around the group, each child taking one cube at a time.

each got four cubes. If we had a knife, we could divide the other one up, and we'd each have a quarter."

Michael's group figured out how many they would each get before dividing the cubes. "We counted and found out we'd each get four. First we counted 1, 2, 3; 1, 2, 3; 1, 2, 3; 1, 2, 3; but there were too many left over. So we counted 1, 2, 3, 4, and that worked with just one extra."

After their explanations, I recorded the problem on the chalkboard with mathematical symbols. I repeated the problem again as I wrote on the chalkboard. "I gave you seventeen cubes to divide among four of you, and you figured out that each person would get four cubes and that there is one cube left over." I wrote: 17 ÷ 4 = 4 R 1. "Who remembers what the 'R' stands for?" I asked.

Several children raised their hands. "The 'R' is the remainder," Patrick answered.

"It's the extra cube," Grace added.

THE MARBLE-SHARING PROBLEM

I posed another problem for the children in this lesson. "This is another sharing problem," I said. "It's more like the five-dollar bill problem. In this problem, the four children who were walking to school found a sack made of shiny red fabric. Inside was a wonderful collection of marbles." We stopped for a moment and discussed their own marble collections. Then I continued.

"The children took the sack to the principal. After a week, she told them that no one had claimed the marbles, so they could have them. She also told them they were to share them equally. When they counted the marbles, they found there were fifty-four in the sack."

I then gave them their task. "Your job is to figure out how to divide fifty-four marbles among four people," I said. I also wrote the problem symbolically on the chalkboard: 54 ÷ 4.

I also wanted the children to record both their answers and the process they used. I gave them directions for doing so. "As with the other problem," I explained, "first, you need to decide upon a plan. Also, one of you needs to be the recorder. The recorder's job is to report what your group does to solve the problem, just as a newspaper reporter writes a story. Your story needs to be complete and should include as many details as possible."

All of the children were able to arrive at the correct answer, but they did so in different ways.

One group of children opted to use the Unifix cubes, as they had for the previous problem. They counted out fifty-four cubes and divided them into four groups. They wrote: *"We think we get 13 each. We think this because we took the cubes and dealt out them one by one. We had two left. Bryce was sick so we gave the extra to him."*

Shaney, Nick, and Gabe wrote the following: *"We had 54. We gave each person 10 because we thout if there was 40 there would be 4 tens and 14 would be left. Each person gets 3 witch leves 2. Each person gets 13."*

These children have not been taught a method for long division and invent their own procedure of first dividing the tens and then the ones.

Tiare recorded for her group: *"We drew 54 marbles and then I numberd them 1, 2, 3, 4 and then we counted the ones and then we knew that each child gets 13 marbes and we lost the other two."*

Jill wrote a report by herself. She was unable to convince Teddy, Grace, and Alana to do it her way, so she wrote her own: *"I wrote down 54. I took away 12. I got 42. I took another 12 away. I got 30. I took another 12 away. I got 18. I took another 12 away. I got 6. Then I took away 4. I got 2. I chiped each of them into halfs that made 4 halfs. Each person got 13 and a half."*

Jill shared her method with the class, but told me later that she was worried that Grace wouldn't be her best friend any more. Later in the day, however, they were skipping and chatting together.

Amber, Vanessa, Ann, and Patrick use a combination of trial and error and addition to arrive at a solution.

BEGINNING THE THIRD LESSON

For this lesson, I planned a series of division problems for the children to solve. My plan was to have them solve the problems concretely, using cubes or tiles, and I would connect each of the problems to the appropriate mathematical notation.

I began the lesson with a class discussion about the division problems we had done in the previous lessons. I did this both to refocus the children on division and to review the mathematical notation I had introduced.

First I wrote $5.00 ÷ 4 on the board and said, "I've used mathematical symbols to write a problem we've already solved. Who can remember the story I told about this problem?"

After a few moments, about a third of the hands were raised. Grace explained clearly, "Four children found a five-dollar bill and had to share it equally."

"Can anyone remember how much each child got?" I asked.

Most hands went up. Nick gave the correct answer, and I completed the mathematical sentence. It now read: $5.00 ÷ 4 = $1.25.

Andreas raised his hand. "We did another problem. We shared fifty cents." He couldn't remember how much they each got, but Alana remembered that they each got twelve cents and that there were two cents left over. I wrote on the board: 50¢ ÷ 4 = 12¢ R 2¢.

"On another day," I continued, "I gave you cubes to use, and this problem to solve." I wrote on the board: 17 ÷ 4. Patrick told the story about sharing the cubes and gave the answer as well. I completed the statement: 17 ÷ 4 = 4 R 1.

"Here's another problem you solved," I said and wrote on the board: 54 ÷ 4. "Who can remember what the story was for this problem?" Jill remembered about the marbles, Laura remembered the answer, and I completed the mathematical sentence: 54 ÷ 4 = 13 R 2.

PRESENTING MORE SHARING PROBLEMS

I went on to the new lesson. "I have seven more problems for you to do today," I told the children. "For each problem, I'll tell you the story, and you will use cubes or tiles to help you solve it. First, I'll distribute the materials."

I had the children work in pairs instead of in groups of four. In that way, though they still had support for their thinking, I felt I could better observe individuals to get an idea of the children's number sense. I gave twenty-five cubes or tiles to each pair.

"For each of these problems, you'll use the cubes or tiles to represent something different. For example, for the first problem, each cube or tile will be a rabbit's ear." I drew a crude version of a rabbit on the board.

I then continued with directions. "Also, you won't need all the cubes or tiles for every problem. For this problem, you and your partner need just fourteen. So count out that many, and push the other cubes or tiles aside for now." I gave the children a chance to do that task.

"When I tell you the problem you are to solve, you and your partner have to agree on a solution. Also, you have to show it with the material you have." I gave this direction because I wanted the children to have the experience of using the cubes or tiles to find or to verify their solutions.

I then gave the first problem. "There was a large cage full of rabbits. I counted all the ears I could see from looking down into the cage. There were fourteen ears. How many rabbits were in the cage?"

As I suspected, a few of the children knew the answer without using the material. Some thought they knew the answer, but weren't correct. Others needed the cubes or tiles to make headway. I observed this, encouraging them all to show their solutions with the material they had. There was lots of discussion among children, some confusion, and a great deal of excitement, all of which I expected with this first problem. All were able to arrive at the correct answer.

Gabe gave the answer he and Nick had found. "There are seven rabbits," he said.

I then asked children to describe how they showed this answer with the cubes or tiles. Gabe said that they put them in twos because each rabbit has two ears. They had a row of seven twos neatly lined up. Timothy and Alana did it differently; each of them took one "ear" for each rabbit. They wound up with seven cubes each.

I then connected the problem to the mathematical sentence and wrote on the board: 14 ÷ 2 = 7. I also wrote the numbers from 1 to 7 on the board and checked off the number 1 to keep track of the problems we were doing.

"Here's the second problem," I said. "This time you'll need twenty cubes or tiles. Push the others aside for now."

When they had done so, I gave the problem. "I have three apple trees in my back yard. Last week, I picked twenty apples and shared them equally among four of my friends. How many apples did each of my friends get?"

Again, there was much discussion and a variety of approaches in the classroom. Most divided their twenty cubes or tiles into four groups, distributing them by ones or by twos.

Shaney and Mairead raise their hands for help about how to share twenty apples among four people.

Shaney and Mairead got into a bit of a jam. They made piles of four tiles each and wound up with five piles. They compared their solution with Nick and Gabe's, who had decided that each person got five apples. The girls were confused and raised their hands for help.

"They say we're wrong," Shaney told me, referring to Nick and Gabe. "See, we got four apples in each pile."

"How many friends got apples?" I asked.

"Four," Shaney and Mairead answered together.

"Show me their shares," I said. They identified four piles and were then confused about their last pile of four tiles.

"What does each tile stand for?" I asked, trying to get to the source of their confusion. They knew that each tile was an apple.

"It looks to me as if you gave each friend four apples," I said, and they agreed. "But it also looks to me," I continued, "as if you've got four extra apples you haven't divided up yet."

"Oh, yeah!" Mairead said, and put another tile on each pile. Shaney still looked confused.

"Your job now," I said to Mairead, "is to explain what you've just done so Shaney can understand. Gabe and Nick, listen to Mairead's explanation to see if you agree." I left the group.

By this time, the others were finished. I brought the class to attention. "Hold up fingers to show me how many apples I gave to each of my friends," I said. This helped to quiet the children and to get them focused on me. We discussed their findings. I recorded "20 ÷ 4 = 5" on the board and checked off number 2. I then asked, "How many more problems do I have for you?" and noticed who raised their hands immediately and who needed to count to figure it out.

"For number 3," I began, "after I tell a story, but before you solve the problem, I'm going to ask you two questions. First I'm going to ask what the cubes or tiles will represent in this problem. Then I'm going to ask how many of your cubes or tiles you'll need." In this way, I was leading the children to solve the problems more independently, without so much of my prompting.

I told the story. "One day it was raining, but not so hard that the children couldn't go out for recess. When they were out, however, some of the children played in a big puddle and got their shoes wet. When they came into class, their teacher told those children with wet shoes to take them off and put them near the heater to dry. The children did as she had said. The teacher counted sixteen shoes near the heater. How many children got their feet wet?"

I then asked my two questions. Though all the children agreed they needed to use sixteen of their cubes or tiles, there was disagreement about whether the materials should represent shoes or children. Michael's explanation seemed to resolve the issue. "The teacher only knew how many wet shoes there were. We have to figure out the children, so the cubes have to be shoes."

Again the children solved the problem and held up fingers to show their answers. This time, I asked what mathematical sentence I should write on the board for this problem. Most hands were raised.

I continued in the same way for the remaining four problems, having the children identify what the cubes or tiles represented, decide how many they needed, and present their solutions. For each, I recorded the matching mathematical sentence on the board.

The fourth problem was: "I was going to my friend's house for a party. She phoned and asked me to buy eighteen cans of Coke for her. How many six-packs did I buy?"

Before presenting problem number 5, I asked the children if they knew how many tennis balls come in a can. Many did, and I had a tennis ball can to show them that it held three balls. I then gave the problem, "Two people were practicing tennis and using lots of balls so they wouldn't have to chase them so often. When they finished, they picked up all the balls they had used and put them back into cans. They had sixteen balls. How many cans did they use?"

The discussion for this problem was interesting, as two different answers were offered. Teddy reported for himself and Grace. He said, "We think they used five cans, and there was one ball left over." Ann explained for herself and Patrick. "We think they used six cans, but one wasn't full." Patrick added some more, "They needed two more balls to fill up the last can."

"Sometimes, there is more than one answer that makes sense," I told the children. I recorded both solutions: $16 \div 3 = 5 \text{ R } 1$ and $16 \div 3 = 6 - 2B$, using "B" to stand for tennis balls.

Problem number 6 had only one solution: "I counted and found that twenty-one days had gone by. How many weeks is that?"

I introduced the seventh problem by drawing a five-pointed star on the board, circling and counting each of the points for the children. Then I presented the problem: "I drew some stars on a piece of paper. When I counted, I found I had 25 points. How many stars did I draw?"

THE FOURTH LESSON

It seemed to me that the number of pencils in the pencil cans on each of the tables was increasing. Children brought new pencils from home, small ones were not discarded, and the collections grew. I decided to use the pencils for another experience with division.

"I'm curious to find out how many pencils you have altogether on your tables," I told the children. I then asked each group to count its pencils and be prepared to report how many there were.

After a few minutes, all the groups were ready to report. I recorded the counts from the seven groups on the chalkboard. The largest number reported was 44; the smallest was 3, from the table with Marina, Kendra, and Bryce, with just one favorite pencil each.

"Each of you add up these numbers," I said, "to see how many pencils there are in all. Then compare your answers in your groups and resolve any differences."

The children got busy. Having them work alone and then compare their answers is a way for children to have an individual experience with the support of their group for verification. It didn't take long for the children to agree that there were 163 pencils in all.

I then presented the division problem. "Suppose we were going to start the new year with empty pencil cans," I told the class. "We'd divide up all the pencils you now have, without worrying about whether the pencils are short ones or long ones, but making sure each of you gets the same number of pencils. So you will divide 163 by 27." I wrote $163 \div 27$ on the chalkboard.

"Your task is to figure out how many pencils each child would get," I said.

The children got to work. Some groups worked on the problem together; other groups worked individually or in pairs and then compared results. The children's methods differed.

Laura, Teddy, and Grace drew twenty-seven circles. They wrote: *"Everyone would get 6 and there would be 1 left over. We figured this out by drawing 27 circles. Grace put talley marks in them while Teddy and Laura counted. We proved it by adding 27 6 times and adding one."*

Kendra, Bryce, and Marina did it in a similar way. They reported: *"We think that each child will get 6 pencils and thre will be 1 left over. We think this because we made a circle for each kid and gave them each five pencils. We added it up. It came to 135 so we took 135 from 163 and there were 28 left. There are 27 kids in the class so each kid gets one more and there is one left."*

Kendra
Bryce
Marina

A math problem about pencils

We think that each child will get 6 pencils and there will be 1 left over. We think this because we made a circle for each kid and and gave them each five pencils. We added it up. It came to 135 so we took 135 from 163 and there were 28 left. There are 27 kids in the class so each kid gets one more and there is one left.

This group uses an estimate first, giving five pencils to each of the twenty-seven children, and then adjusts their solution.

In a group in which the children worked separately, Tiare used a different approach. Rather than divide 163 into twenty-seven groups, she divided 163 into groups of twenty-seven. She wrote: *"I think that each child will get six penicles because I wrote a chart. I made 163 numbers by sumbolys. At first I made lines. I crossed out 27 lines now each person gets one penicle. Next I did circlirs now each person gets 2 penicles. Next I did X's then S's then R's D's. It came out so that each child will get 6 penicles and there is one R."*

Erika, also in her group, did it the same way as reported by the two first groups. Andreas and Tara worked together, starting with 163 and subtracting 27. They did this several times, and then got bogged down in their calculations and lost sight of where they were going. They abandoned their work unfinished and joined forces with Erika.

Gabe, Nick, Shaney, and Mairead worked together. They used Unifix cubes, carefully counting out 163, grouping them by tens. They were stumped about how to continue, and spent a great deal of time trying to get the cubes into twenty-seven equal shares. They finally did it, but enough cubes had been lost in the shuffle and were under the table that they reported that each child would get five pencils and that there would be a remainder of twenty. They were surprised and a bit dismayed to hear the others' answers.

From listening to one another's methods, children had the opportunity to hear about different approaches to solving division problems. It is from solving problems such as these over time that children will learn about situations that call for division and how to deal with them.

Tiare organizes the numerals from 1 to 163 into groups of twenty-seven each.

Developing Understanding of Place Value

Understanding place value requires that children learn several ideas. When first experiencing place value, children are presented with the new idea of making groups of tens and then counting groups as if they were single items. This means that they have to learn to think about a group of ten as being simultaneously one entity and made up of ten individual objects.

In addition, this idea is connected to the symbolism for numbers. Though our place-value system is a marvelous one, allowing us to represent any number with just ten digits, this system is not simple for children to understand. They must learn that digits have different values, depending on their positions in numbers. The difference between 36 and 63, for example, though obvious to adults, may be subtle for children.

To help children develop understanding of place value, teachers need to give them varied experiences. The children need to work with concrete materials that they can group into tens and hundreds. They need to work with problem situations that call for analyzing large numbers of things. They need to learn to link their concrete experiences to the standard symbolization for numbers.

Also, children need these types of experiences over time. Though some young children can count well into the hundreds, that does not necessarily mean that they understand the structure underlying those numbers. Though some children have learned that 27, for example, is made of two tens and seven ones, they do not necessarily relate those facts to the quantity that number represents. Though some children have learned to group objects by tens and to use that information to record the number, when given a large quantity of objects to count, they still resort to counting by ones instead of grouping. Time and experience are needed for children to see grouping into tens as a useful organizer for making sense of large numbers.

Several types of experiences are presented in this section to help children learn about place value. Chapter 6 presents lessons in which children use the ideas of making and counting groups. Chapter 7 describes a collection of activities organized for children's independent work. Chapter 8 suggests ways to use a specific manipulative material, Base Ten Blocks, to help children learn about grouping by tens.

Chapter 6
Making Tens and Ones

When learning about place value, children benefit from experiences in which they organize objects into groups of ten to count how many there are. This chapter presents two separate activities in which the opportunity for grouping by tens was an organizational tool for making sense out of numbers.

In the first activity, first graders investigated the number of pockets there are altogether in the class. In the second activity, second graders estimated how many beans fill a pill bottle, and then counted to check their predictions. Each activity is appropriate for helping children in grades 1, 2, and 3 learn about the structure and usefulness of place value. In addition, these activities are useful for preparing children for the independent work on the menu described in Chapter 7.

HOW MANY POCKETS?

"How many pockets do you think we are wearing today altogether?" I asked the class on Monday morning. These were first graders. I was interested in providing the children with an opportunity to estimate and compare numbers that would also contribute to their experience with place value. To do so, I planned this concrete experience to build their number understanding and present how we use the concept of grouping by tens for larger numbers.

I gave the children a few minutes to consider the question of how many pockets they had. Some started to count the pockets on their own clothes. Mark was especially excited. "I've got ten just on my jeans!" he shouted. He was wearing jeans that had pockets everywhere.

Melissa went and put on her jacket. "I have more pockets this way," she announced to the others at her table. They saw this as a good idea also, and went to get their jackets. However, I asked that all children leave their jackets in their cubbies. Melissa reluctantly returned hers.

I asked the children for estimates. Responses varied. "Maybe a hundred." "Fifty." "Lots." "I bet there's more than a hundred."

I then organized a way for the class to find out how many pockets there really were. "I'm going to put a supply of Unifix cubes at each table," I told the children. "Then I want each of you to put one Unifix cube in each of your pockets." I demonstrated for the children by placing a cube in each of the six I had—two in my skirt, one in my blouse, and three in my jacket.

"When each of you has put one cube in each of your pockets," I continued, "I'll come and collect the extras. Then I'll give some more directions."

The children put one Unifix cube in each of their pockets.

I distributed cubes to each table. The children put cubes in their pockets, and I collected the remaining cubes. I then gave further directions.

"Watch what I do with the cubes in my pockets," I said to the children. I removed my six cubes and snapped them into a train. I had the children count how many I had with me. "Each of you should now do the same with the cubes in your pockets," I explained. "Then compare your trains with one another at your table."

The children had made their trains almost before I had completed giving directions. As I circulated, I listened to the language they were using to compare their trains. "I have most." "My train has more than yours." "Mine is tallest." "Yours is the smallest." "Mine has mostest." "Look, you have five, and I have six. Mine's bigger."

I called the children back to attention. "I'm going to make some statements," I told the children. "Listen carefully to what I say. Then check with the person next to you to see if the statement fits you. If it does, hold your Unifix train up for me to see." For more than half the children in the class, English was not their first language. I used every opportunity I could to connect their activity to appropriate language.

"If you have six cubes in your train, hold it up," I said. Some children immediately showed their trains. I reminded them that they were to check with the person sitting next to them before doing so. Checking with another would help those for whom the language was difficult.

"Hold up your train if you have more than four pockets," I said next. I had the children who held up trains call out how many cubes they had.

"If you have fewer than five pockets, hold up your train," I said next. I had to say this in another way for some of the children. "That means your train has fewer than five cubes."

I continued with others. "If you have more than two cubes, hold up your train." "Hold up your train if someone else at your table has one the same length." "Hold up your train if yours is the shortest at the table." "Who thinks he or she has the least number of pockets in the whole class?" (Nancy didn't have any pockets and had felt a little left out. She seemed thrilled to be able to respond to this last question.)

I then switched to another activity. "Now we're going to find out how many pockets we have altogether," I said. "To do that, see if you can make a train of ten from the cubes at your table. If you have enough, make more trains of ten. When you've done that, I'll ask each group to report how many tens and ones you have altogether."

I had the children bring their tens to the front of the room. Then I had the groups, one by one, bring up their extra cubes. I used their extra cubes to make trains of ten, counting out loud and encouraging the children to count with me. "I have four from Hassan's table. Tina's table has three extras. Let's count: four, five, six, seven. Jennifer, bring up your table's extras."

I stood the trains of ten on the chalkboard tray. I had the children count the trains by tens with me, and then count the extra cubes by ones. There were sixty-eight in all. "I'll record this, and then we'll try it again tomorrow," I told the class. I set up a chart on the chalkboard.

How many pockets do we have?

Monday 6 tens and 8 ones = 68
Tuesday
Wednesday
Thursday
Friday

We continued the activity throughout the week. The children came wearing more pockets on Tuesday, motivated to increase the Monday count. (Mark wore the same jeans again.) There were 82 pockets. The count rose to 87 on Wednesday and to 95 on Thursday. (Mark was still wearing the same jeans.) The children were hoping for 100 on Friday. However, they were disappointed. The Friday count was only 89. Obviously, the children had exhausted the pocket potential of their wardrobes by the end of the week. (Mark no longer wore the same jeans. "My mother wouldn't let me," he explained.)

ESTIMATING BEANS

To prepare for this activity with second graders, I filled small, clear pill bottles, all of which were the same size, with lima beans. The children sat in groups of six, and I prepared five such bottles, one for each group. I showed the class one of the bottles and said, "Make an estimate of how many beans you think there are in this container."

The children's estimates ranged from ten to twenty-eight. I wrote each on the chalkboard as it was reported.

"What was the smallest estimate made?" I asked.

"Ten," a chorus of children said.

"What is next smallest?" I asked.

"Fifteen." "Twelve." "It's twelve."

I continued in this way, rewriting their estimates into a list on the board from smallest to largest, writing only once each that had been given.

10
12
15
17
20
21
25
26
27
28

"I'm going to give each group a container filled with beans that is the same size as this one," I continued. "When you have your group's container, look at it closely, but don't open it. See what you can figure out just by looking in from the outside and, as a group, agree on an estimate of how many beans there are inside. I want just one estimate from each group." I passed out the containers to the groups.

Within five minutes, all but two groups had agreed upon an estimate. One of those remaining two groups was close to coming to a group decision; the other group was far from the goal and did not appear to be moving closer. I told them they had just one minute more to come to agreement.

Because this was the first such experience for the children, I was not surprised at the difficulty this group was having. I planned to take the time and have groups describe the processes they used for coming to consensus. I would use their descriptions to focus the class on different ways that groups can come to decisions.

The first group that reported had made an estimate of twenty-eight. "Did you all agree on this number at first?" I asked.

"All of us but Joshua," Heather replied.

"What happened that made you agree, Joshua?" I asked.

"They talked me into it," Joshua answered.

"Did they do something or explain something to convince you?" I probed.

"They just talked me into it," Joshua explained.

Without opening the container, the group has to agree on an estimate of how many beans are inside.

I recorded 28 on the chalkboard, and asked for another group's estimate.

Next, Reem reported for her group. "We were stuck on two answers, either forty or fifty," she said. "Then we decided to agree on forty-nine." I wrote 49 on the chalkboard.

The third group reported an estimate of thirty-seven. When I asked them how they had come to agreement on that estimate, Daniel confessed, "When you said we only had one more minute, it was easier to agree." I wrote 37.

The fourth group that reported was the one that was having the most difficulty coming to a consensus. They had narrowed their estimate down to two choices. Edward reported, "We think it is either twenty-nine or fifty." I wrote both 29 and 50 on the chalkboard and went to the last group.

Heather reported that her group's estimate was thirty. "Can you explain how your group agreed on that estimate?" I asked.

The children in the group looked at one another. All were silent. Finally Brian spoke. "We just did," he said, shrugging. It is not always easy for children to verbalize their processes, so this response did not surprise me. I wrote 30 on the chalkboard.

In the meantime, the group that had not reached agreement had continued to work, even though they were supposed to be listening to the others report. Miho raised her hand. "We think it's twenty-nine," she said.

"Do you want me to erase the 50?" I asked.

"Yes," Miho responded.

"Is that okay with your whole group?" I asked.

The other children in the group responded by nodding or orally giving their assent. I erased the 50.

"Let's list your group estimates in order from smallest to largest," I said. I had the children help with this task, and wrote the new list of five numbers next to the original list of ten guesses.

First estimates	Second estimates
10	28
12	29
15	30
17	37
20	49
21	
25	
26	
27	
28	

"What is different about these two lists?" I asked.

"There's less in the new list," Stacy said.

"Why do you think that is so?" I asked.

"Because the second time we could give only one guess for a group," Rebecca answered.

Philip raised his hand. "The new estimates are higher," he said.

"Why do you think that is?" I asked.

Philip shrugged, but Daniel had a thought. "When we got a closer look," he said, "we could see more." There were no other comments offered.

"Each group is going to count the beans in the container you have," I told the children, "but I want you to do the counting in a special way. Open your container, carefully pour out the beans, and then arrange them in some way that would make it easy for someone to count how many you have."

The children did this quickly. Two groups put the beans into piles of five: one group had six piles with one extra bean; the other had six piles with two extra beans. One group made three groups of ten, with two extra beans. Another group made three neat rows with ten in each and had four extra beans. The group that had had difficulty coming to consensus struggled to share their beans so they each had the same amount. Each finally wound up with five beans, and there was one extra, which they left in the middle. I recorded their counts on the board: 31, 31, 32, 34, 34.

Philip raised his hand. "Too bad no one got thirty-three," he said. His own need for order would have been satisfied if that gap didn't exist in the counts.

"The pill containers I used were all the same size," I said, "and I filled them all full. Why did groups come up with different numbers when you counted?"

The children had several thoughts about this. "You didn't shake them down." "The beans aren't all the same size." "You didn't fill them all the same."

I then related their experience with the beans to place value. "When you arranged your beans, some of you made groups of ten and some of you made groups of five. Making the same size groups is helpful for keeping track of large numbers of things. The number system we use is based on grouping by tens."

I then gave several small paper cups to each group, the kind used for pills in hospitals. I also gave each group a 9-inch-by-12-inch piece of tag folded in half, with the left half labeled Tens and the right half labeled Ones.

I then gave the directions to the class: "Using the beans from your container, fill as many cups as you can, putting exactly ten beans in each cup. Place the full cups on the left side, the Tens side, of your board; place any extra beans on the right side, the Ones side."

The children did this quickly. The groups reported how many tens and how many ones they had. For each, I drew a sketch of the tag on the chalkboard, labeling the left side of it "Tens" and the right side "Ones." I recorded their information. I had the children read what I had recorded from each group in two ways, as three tens and four ones, for example, and also as thirty-four.

Though it might have been valuable for the children to have seen how many beans the groups had altogether by combining their tens and ones, and grouping tens into a larger cup to introduce hundreds, I decided that the children had had enough for that day and collected the materials.

ADDITIONAL SUGGESTIONS

Many opportunities arise for grouping objects into tens and ones in the class, often as incidental aspects of other activities or investigations. It's beneficial to take advantage of such opportunities so children come to see our place-value system of organization as a way of making sense of numbers.

Graphing experiences are useful for this. For example, a field trip to the local children's museum was planned for a class of second graders. In preparation for the trip, the children reported by marking an X on a graph to indicate whether they had visited the museum before.

Have you visited the children's museum before?
Mark an X.
YES   X   X   X   X   X   X   X   X   X
NO   X   X   X   X   X   X   X   X   X   X   X   X   X   X   X   X   X

When counting the Xs, it helped to circle ten of the Xs in the second row to see that there was one ten and seven extras.

When summarizing the results of their spinner experiments (see Chapter 14), second graders taped their results on the chalkboard, combining their strips of 1s, 2s, and 3s to make strips that stretched well across the room. To find out how many were in each row, it helped to mark each row by tens, count by tens, and then add the extras.

To count the books in the class library, a group of second graders put the books into piles of ten each. To find out how many field-trip permission slips had been returned, a small committee put them into groups of ten and reported how many groups and extras there were. The children responsible for putting out the cups for juice during snack time can be asked to line them up in rows of ten, with an additional row of extras, so I can more easily see how many cups there are. From repeated experiences over time, children's understanding of place value will grow.

Chapter 7
A Place-Value Menu

This chapter reports second graders' experiences with a collection of activities that focused on place value. The activities were organized into a unit called a *menu*. Initially, there were seven activities on the menu; three additional activities were added later to the unit for those children who finished more quickly. All of the tasks that were presented are reproduced at the end of the chapter.

The children worked in pairs. Though they had to complete all the tasks, they were able to choose the order in which to do them. The classroom was organized so there were eight designated stations at which children worked. Each station was a cluster of four or six desks, or an available table, and was marked by a sign suspended above it from the ceiling, labeling it triangle, square, circle, heart, or other shape.

The materials for each activity were placed in rubber dish tubs that were labeled to match the labels of the stations. The tubs contained the manipulatives needed for the activity; the task sheet, written on ditto paper and placed in a sturdy sleeve made of acetate on one side and cardboard on the other; and a holder for propping up the task sheet so the children could read it easily. The tubs were stored on the bookshelves and when it was time for work on the menu, assigned monitors carried them to their stations and set up the materials.

GETTING ORGANIZED

When introducing the menu tasks, I gave the children specific directions for what I expected—how the monitors should set out the materials, how the children were to do each activity, and how they were to record their results. For the games on the menu—the Five-Tower Game and Digit Place—I played sample games with the class and modeled how they should record in their record books. For other activities, I made sure to introduce all the skills called for. In the activity called Stars, for example, children needed to be able to draw stars and to time one minute. I practiced these with the class.

I presented and discussed each menu task carefully. Though this was time consuming, it was valuable for minimizing the clarifications that most likely would be needed later.

Besides writing the tasks and collecting the materials, I made a recording booklet for each child, using 12-inch-by-18-inch construction paper for covers and inserting eight sheets of 9-inch-by-12-inch newsprint. In addition, I included a piece of lined paper on which the children were to copy the menu tasks from the list I had prepared and posted. In front of each task, they were to draw the symbol used for the station where that task would be put—a triangle, square, circle, heart, or other shape.

The children pasted this "shape" sheet in the inside cover of their booklets. When they finished a task, they would color in the symbol they had drawn. This helped each child keep track of what was completed and also made it easy for me to glance into the children's booklets to get a sense of their progress.

To introduce the menu, I planned to spend one class period teaching the children how to play the game Digit Place, and then introducing a few of the other tasks. On the second day, I would review the game and play it again with the class. Then I would introduce the remaining tasks and give the children the remainder of the period to begin work.

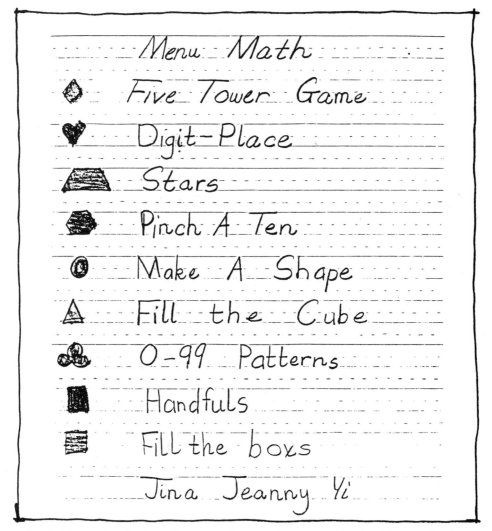

The children copy the list of menu tasks into their recording booklets and color in the symbols as they finish.

I decided on this plan for several reasons. I felt that teaching the rules for Digit Place on one day, and then reinforcing them the next day would be helpful. Also, I felt it was better to avoid giving directions for seven different activities at one time. In addition, I've come to learn that the initial work time on a menu has logistic difficulties; allowing just half a period gave me adequate time to identify difficulties and note clarifications needed.

TEACHING DIGIT PLACE AND INTRODUCING THE TASKS

To teach Digit Place, I had the children gather on the rug at the back of the room. I find it helpful to have the children seated on the rug because there they are removed from distractions on their desks. Also, because the children are sitting more closely together, I believe it is easier for me to monitor their attention and participation.

"I'm going to teach you a game," I said when they were settled. "It is a guessing game. I'll pick a number, and you'll try to guess what it is. The number I pick will have two digits in it. You'll make guesses by telling me a two-digit number. Then I will tell you how many of the digits in your number are correct and how many of those are in the correct place."

I asked, "Who can give an example of a two-digit number?" Several children offered examples. "50." "17." "84." I wrote each on the board.

When I called on Edward, he said, "99." I wrote it on the board.

"I'm glad you suggested that number, Edward," I said. "That reminds me of an important rule for this game. You cannot use a double-digit number, one with both digits the same. So aside from 99, what other numbers can't be used?"

The children called out others. "55." "33." And so on.

"What does *digit* mean?" I asked, to check their understanding.

"It means number," Angie answered. Other children nodded in agreement.

"*Two digits* means two numbers," Brian added.

I then gave an explanation of how the game is played. "Suppose the number I picked was 17. In a real game, I wouldn't tell you this, but I did this time just for practice." I wrote "17" on the board and circled it. I also drew a line to make two columns, writing "digit" at the top of the left-hand column and "place" at the top of the right-hand column.

"Now suppose that someone guesses 74," I continued. "I would tell you that 74 has one correct digit, but no correct place." I wrote this on the chart.

	digit	*place*
74	1	0

"Who can explain why I said 74 has one correct digit?" I asked. Several children raised their hands, and I gave all who volunteered the chance to explain. Verbalizing their thoughts is important. Even when children have the same idea, there is benefit from giving as many as possible the chance to

When playing Digit Place, the children use the clues to help them guess the number.

explain their thinking. This gives more children the experience of expressing their ideas and gives the others a variety of responses to hear. Very often children's wording differs for the same thought.

"Who can explain why I wrote zero in the place column?" I asked. Again, several children offered explanations.

I then played a real game with the children. I chose the number 42 and wrote it on a slip of paper. This was to model for the children that they were to write their number when they played the game with one another. Writing the number avoids the problem of a child's forgetting it in the midst of the guessing.

Heather made the first guess, "16." I started a new chart and wrote zeros in both columns.

"What do you now know?" I asked.

"There's no 1 or 6 in your number," Philip answered.

Daniel made the second guess, "84." I wrote a 1 in the digit column and a 0 in the place column.

"What do you now know?" I asked again.

"There's either an 8 or a 4 in your number," Reem said.

"You don't know which one, but you know it's not in the right place," Daniel added.

I continued, recording the children's guesses. After I responded to each guess, I asked the children to tell what they now knew. The children guessed the number on their eighth try.

	digit	place
16	0	0
84	1	0
79	0	0
89	0	0
47	1	1
43	1	1
41	1	1
42	2	2

The children enjoyed the game and were anxious to play again. I told them they would have the chance to play with their partners on the menu, and spent the rest of the math time introducing two other menu activities.

The next day, I introduced the four remaining tasks. At this time, I did not introduce the extra tasks. Seven different activities seemed enough for the children at this time. I chose the monitors for the stations and organized the children into partners. The monitors took the tubs to the stations and set up the materials. They were used to this system and did the setting up quickly and efficiently.

Once the materials were in place, I reminded the children about some of the operating principles necessary. "Remember, you and your partner are to work together. You can choose any task you like to begin, and you can do the tasks in whatever order you'd like."

I then presented the children with a potential problem. "What will you do if the station where you were planning to go is full, with children in all the available chairs?" I asked.

The children offered several different responses. "You have to choose another." "You wait until there is a space." "But in the meantime, you go somewhere else." With seven tasks, there were more than forty places, enough places so children would be likely to get their choices. When I introduced the extra tasks, there would be even more options.

I then asked each pair of partners to talk and decide where they thought they'd like to go first. As partners raised their hands and reported the task they would like to try first, I dismissed them to go and begin work. The children filtered throughout the room and got started on their tasks.

The guesses of 15 and 19 are not necessary as the first and fourth clues indicate that neither 5 nor 9 is possible.

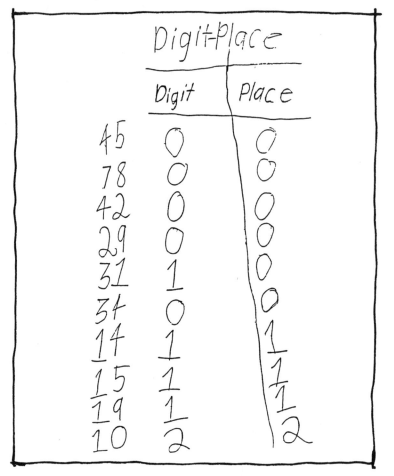

DURING THE WORK TIME

The children approached their work enthusiastically and with purpose. They were careful about how they followed directions and how they recorded in their booklets. However, several rough edges were evident during this beginning work period.

On three of the tasks—Stars, Pinch a Ten, and Fill the Cube—children were asked to record predictions, then to do the activity, and then to compare their predictions to their actual counts. I noticed that a few of the children were disturbed by the discrepancy between their predictions and the actual counts, and were busily erasing to make changes in their books. I made a note to discuss this with the class at the beginning of the next period.

The directions on Make a Shape were confusing. I decided that I would discuss the directions with the children and have them help me reword them so they more clearly explained what to do.

Only two children elected to play Digit Place in this first work time. I didn't know if that was because they weren't comfortable with the game or if they were curious about the other tasks. I made a note to play another game with the class.

Even with these difficulties, the interaction between children was exciting to watch. One pair of children were coloring in the pattern of the even numbers on the 0–99 chart. Edward noticed quickly that the even numbers went in stripes, and was coloring down the columns. "My pattern looks like a purple zebra," he said. His partner, Stacy, however, had her own approach. She was coloring in the numbers in order, 2, 4, 6, 8, 10, 12, and so on. Though she kept glancing over at Edward's paper, she methodically continued as she had begun. It wasn't until Stacy had colored in almost three-fourths of her sheet that she felt secure to change her method and color in the numbers by columns.

Both children, however, had left zero uncolored, and I talked with them about that, pointing out both that zero fit the pattern of the stripes and that every other number that ended in zero was even. I also showed them how all the even numbers could be written as the sum of two of the same addends, which included zero since it could be written as 0 + 0. Edward seemed to be comfortable with this; Stacy wasn't convinced.

When working on Fill the Cube, the children had to predict how many of both popcorn kernels and lentils it would take to fill a Unifix cube. After

For the task of Stars, children make a prediction, do the activity, and record their actual count.

making her guess for popcorn, Rebecca commented to her partner, "It looks like it takes two lentils to make a piece of popcorn." She went back to thinking about how to use that information in her prediction for lentils.

Before the children went back to work the next day, I gathered them together. I had them participate in the rewording of the confusing task. I discussed why it was okay that there were differences between predictions and counts. I played another game of Digit Place with them.

Work continued more smoothly over the next several days. After four days, I introduced Handfuls and Fill the Boxes, two of the additional tasks. They added a bit of new interest for the children. Angie, however, was unimpressed. "Fill, fill, fill," she said, "all we ever do is fill." Hers did not seem to be a majority position, however.

Several days after that, I explained the Number Puzzle activity to the children, the last activity I had prepared for this menu. "As with the two other new tasks," I told the children, "this task is not required. It is something extra that you can do if you like when you have completed all the other activities."

Following the directions propped at the station, Miho and Danny test whether thirty-two tiles will cover their shape.

All in all, the children worked for about two weeks on this menu. During that time, they stayed involved with the activities. When they completed their work, partners had the responsibility to read each other's recording booklets and suggest changes or corrections that could be made to improve their work. In this way, they had a chance to revisit all the tasks before the unit was over.

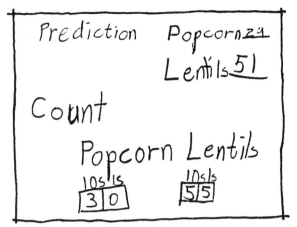

In Fill the Cube, children put kernels of popcorn and lentils into groups of ten to count how many of each fill a Unifix cube.

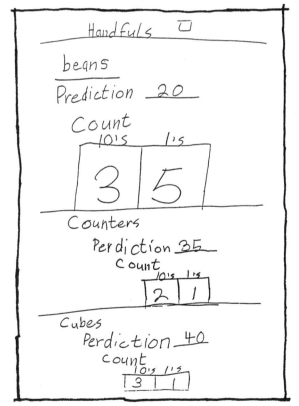

In the Handfuls task, children are encouraged to use the information from each handful they count for the next prediction.

These are the directions the children use for the Place Value menu tasks.

Five Tower Game

You need: Unifix cubes
2 dice
a partner

Do: Roll the dice and take that many cubes. Snap them into a tower. Take turns doing this until you each have 5 towers.

Snap your 5 towers together. Compare with your partner. Break your long train into 10s and record.

Record:

Names

10s	1s		10s	1s

Write who has more and who has less.

Digit Place

You need: a partner

Do: One person picks a 2-digit number. (The digits should be different.) The other person tries to guess the number. For each guess, the first person tells how many digits in the guess are correct and how many of the correct digits are in the correct place.

A chart helps:

Guess	Digit	Place
27	0	0
13	1	1

Do not tell which digit is correct — just how many.

Play again with the other person guessing this time.

☆ Stars ☆

You need: a partner
a way to time 1 minute

Predict: How many stars do you think you can draw in 1 minute? Write your prediction in your notebook.

Do: Make stars while your partner times 1 minute.

Count: Circle groups of 10 stars. How many 10s? How many 1s? Record in your notebook.

Extend: Repeat. What would you do to get better results? Write this in your notebook.

Pinch a Ten

You need: kidney beans

Predict: If you take 10 pinches of beans, how many times can you pinch exactly 10? Write your prediction in your notebook.

Do: Take a pinch and count. Was your pinch less than, more than, or exactly 10? Do this 10 times.

Record: (Tally like this ╫╫ ll.)

Less than 10	10	More than 10

Extend: Repeat and see if you get better at pinching 10s. Or pinch popcorn.

Make a Shape

You need: a crayon
Color Tiles
a partner
white paper

On the white paper, draw a shape that you both think can be covered with 32 tiles.

Use 10 tiles of one color, then 10 of another, and so on, until your shape is covered. Record the number of tiles you used.

Now draw another shape that you both think can be covered with 32 tiles. Again, cover, count, and record.

Tape or staple your shapes in your notebooks. (Put one in each of your books.)

Fill the Cube

You need: a Unifix cube
popcorn
lentils

Predict: How many kernels of popcorn do you think will fill the cube? Record in your notebook.

Do: Fill the cube. Put the popcorn into piles of 10. How many 10s? How many 1s? Record.

Repeat: Now do this with lentils.

Record:

| Prediction: Popcorn ___ |
| Lentils ___ |

Count:

| Popcorn | Lentils |
| 10s 1s | 10s 1s |

0-99 Patterns

You need: 0-99 charts
crayon
directions (in envelope)
partner

Pick a strip from the envelope. With your partner, read the directions and decide which numbers to color. (Each colors on your own sheet.)

Tape your chart in your notebook. Write a description of the pattern.

Pick another strip and do the same.

Directions

Color all the even numbers.

Color all the numbers with double digits.

Color all the numbers with digits that add to 8.

Color all the numbers with first digits larger than second digits.

Color all numbers that have a 4.

0	1	2	3	4	5	6	7	8	9
10	11	12	13	14	15	16	17	18	19
20	21	22	23	24	25	26	27	28	29
30	31	32	33	34	35	36	37	38	39
40	41	42	43	44	45	46	47	48	49
50	51	52	53	54	55	56	57	58	59
60	61	62	63	64	65	66	67	68	69
70	71	72	73	74	75	76	77	78	79
80	81	82	83	84	85	86	87	88	89
90	91	92	93	94	95	96	97	98	99

Handfuls

You need: Place Value board
beans ♡
cubes ⬜
counters ●
small cups

Predict: How many beans do you think you can hold in a handful? Record in your notebook.

Do: Take a handful.

Count: Use cups to group the beans into 10s. Put your cups on the place value board, along with the extra beans.

Record:

> Handfuls - Beans
> Prediction: _____
> Count: 10s | 1s
> [|]

Repeat: Do the same for cubes and counters.

Fill the Boxes

You need: Unifix cubes
boxes

Predict: Choose one box. Predict how many Unifix cubes can fit inside so that the cover can be put on. Record your prediction in your notebook.

Do: Fill the box.

Count: Snap the cubes into trains of 10. Count 10s and 1s. Record.

Repeat: Do the same for the other 2 boxes.

Box A	Box B	Box C
Prediction ___	Prediction ___	Prediction ___
Count	Count	Count
10s 1s	10s 1s	10s 1s

Number Puzzle

You need: paper with 100 squares
(10 x 10)
scissors
envelope

Write the numbers from 0 to 99 on the squared paper to make a 0-99 chart.

Cutting only on lines, cut the chart into 7 interesting pieces. Write your name on the back on each piece.

Put the pieces in an envelope. Write your name on the envelope.

Try and put your puzzle together. Then place it in the puzzle box.

Choose someone else's puzzle to put together. Sign your name on the back of the envelope to show you solved it.

Chapter 8
Activities with Base Ten Blocks

Base Ten Blocks provide a structural model of our place-value system. From engaging in activities using the blocks, children learn to exchange ten of each block for the next larger block. These experiences prepare them for understanding how and why regrouping is used in standard arithmetic algorithms. Also, the activities help develop children's number sense and ability to compute mentally.

The activities described in this chapter were done with second graders near the end of the school year and third graders in the beginning of the year. Some activities were games that provided experience with exchanging; in other activities, children used the blocks to solve problems.

When introducing the blocks to the children, the names *unit, long,* and *flat* were used instead of *one, ten,* and *hundred*. This was done purposely to keep the children's focus on the concrete material. The word *ten* is likely to trigger the symbolic image of 10, a 1 and a 0. The word *long,* however, describes the material without the symbolic intereference, allowing children to think about our number system concretely. The goal is for them eventually to connect symbolic representations to the concrete materials.

The children also use place-value boards, which serve as organizers for the blocks. These boards indicate places for the children to put the units, longs, and flats that correspond to the positions of 1s, 10s, and 100s as used symbolically.

As with any new material, children need time for free exploration. This time is necessary not only for preparing children to give their attention to more structured activities, it is also valuable time during which they can discover relationships among the blocks. Before they begin any of the activities described, the children should know that it takes ten of one block to make the next larger one.

RACE FOR A FLAT

I introduced this game after time was allowed for the children's free exploration and after a discussion about the relationship of the blocks to one another. "I'm going to teach you a game that you'll play in your groups," I told the children. "You'll use the blocks you've been exploring and a pair of dice. Also, each of you will have a board to use."

I held up a board for the children to see. "Notice that there are three columns on the board," I said. "Each size of block has its own space." I showed them that the units go in the right column, the longs in the center, and the flats on the left.

"The winner of the game is the person who gets a flat first," I continued. "I'm going to show you how to play by demonstrating the game with Chris, Jason, Bayard, and Brandie." I had the children gather around to watch. I gave each of the four children a place-value board, and put out a supply of units, longs, and flats for them to use.

"You take turns rolling the dice," I explained. "Whatever number comes up tells you how many units to put onto your board. I'll let Brandie roll first." Brandie rolled a six, counted six units, and put them on her board.

"Now, Brandie, pass the dice to Chris so he can roll," I said. Chris rolled a three. Before he had counted his units, Bayard reached for the dice. I interrupted them and asked Bayard to return the dice to Chris. I explained why.

"It's important that you leave the dice after they have been rolled until people finish their turns," I said. "This way, there won't be any confusion about what has been rolled. Also, your job is to watch as other people take their turns to make sure you agree with what they are doing. When Chris finishes his turn, then he should pass the dice to the next player." I have found this procedure to be very helpful for focusing the children's attention on what the player is doing and for helping keep the play orderly.

Bayard rolled eleven on his turn. This gave me the chance to introduce another rule of the game. Bayard counted out eleven units. "Before you pass the dice to Jason," I said, "I want to tell you the other rule for this game. Whenever you have enough of one size of block to exchange for another, you must do so."

We had already discussed the exchanging of ten of one size of block for the next larger block. "How many units does it take to make a long?" I asked. The children answered "ten" in unison.

I showed Bayard how to do the exchange. I directed him to take a long, line up ten of the units against it, and then keep the long and return the units to the central supply. He did that and then passed the dice to Jason.

Jason rolled a five, counted the blocks, placed them on his board, and passed the dice to Brandie. This time Brandie rolled eight. After she added eight units to her board, I had her exchange ten of them for a long, using the same procedure I had shown Bayard.

"How do you win?" Michael asked.

"You keep taking turns like this," I said, "until one person is able to exchange enough longs to get a flat." Michael nodded.

"How many longs will you need for that?" I asked. Again, the children answered "ten" in unison. I then asked the other children to take their seats, and asked if there were any questions. There were several.

"Do we have to exchange, or can we save our small blocks?" Jill wanted to know.

"If you have enough blocks to exchange, then you must do so," I said. "You can help one another in your group by asking, 'Do you have anything you can exchange?' before the next person goes."

"Do you have to get exactly a flat, or can you go over?" Amber asked.

"Whoever is first to get at least a flat wins. It's okay if you have more," I answered.

When playing Race for a Flat, each child makes all the exchanges possible before passing the dice to the next player.

"Suppose you roll a ten," Patrick asked. "Do you have to count out the little ones, or can you take one of these?" He held up a long.

"You can take a shortcut like that only if everyone in your group understands what you are doing and agrees with you," I responded. I never tell the children about such shortcuts. That is not something I "teach." I want them to discover shortcuts from their own experience while playing the game, and on their own individual timetables. As the children play, I learn about their understanding by watching to see which children have discovered shortcuts such as Patrick suggested and which children need to count out all the units at each turn.

There were no more questions. I asked that one person from each group get a supply of blocks and a board for each player. The children then began to play.

As with most new activities, there was confusion. Some groups got bogged down deciding who would go first, second, and so on. I mediated in several of

Activities with Base Ten Blocks   85

these squabbles. Other groups got confused about the rules or about exchanging and needed clarification.

The children played for the rest of the period, and then again the next day. Before they got started on the second day, however, I had a discussion with them about deciding who goes first. "When you played the game yesterday," I said, "I noticed that groups used different ways for deciding who should go first, second, third, and last. I'd like each group to tell how you decided, so we can hear about different ways to make that decision."

Children often need help when learning to work together cooperatively. A discussion such as this one deals with one skill of cooperating in the context of the activity they're doing. It's worth the time to focus on issues such as this one. The better children work together, the more smoothly the classroom runs and, I believe, the more supportive the atmosphere is for learning.

Michelle reported for her group. "We rolled the dice and whoever got the highest number went first," she said.

"What about who went second, third, and fourth?" I asked.

Michelle shrugged, and Timmy explained. "We just went around the table this way," he said, indicating with his arm.

Erika raised her hand. "We just called out first, second, third, and fourth, and did it that way," she reported.

Tiare, also in Erika's group, raised her hand. "That wasn't fair," she complained. "If you don't shout out fast, you don't get to go first."

"Let's hear from others," I said, "and then maybe your group can choose another way to decide."

"We take turns in our group," Grace said. "One person goes first this time, and then someone else next time, like that."

"We do it that way too," Gabe reported.

Kendra reported for her group. "Whoever wins gets to go first the next time," she said.

"What about who goes first to begin?" I asked.

"It doesn't matter," she said. "We all get turns."

There were no other ideas. Before having the children get the materials for the game, I asked that they discuss how they were going to decide who would go first, second, and so on. "I'd like you to find a way that satisfies everyone in your group," I said. "When you've decided, then choose someone to come and get your materials."

The second day of play went much more smoothly because the children were more comfortable with the logistics of play. Because of that, I was better able this day to observe and listen to children as they played. While many still counted out the units each time, I saw some children use more efficient methods.

For example, Marina had three units on her board when she rolled a nine. She just took one unit from the three she had, replaced it to the "bank," and took a long. Yet, later, when she had five units on her board and rolled a six, she needed to count out the five units and then exchange.

Many of the children compared their progress as they played. They did this in different ways. Some described who was ahead by referring to the blocks. "Teddy's winning. He has five longs, and that's the most." "I only need two more longs." "If I get a seven, then I'll get another long, and then I'll only need one more long to win."

Other children used numbers whem comparing. "You have fifty-four, and I only have forty-six." "I need twenty-three to win." "You have twelve more than I do."

The true benefit of having children work in small heterogeneous groups was evident to me as I observed the groups. Though children showed different levels of understanding when they exchanged the blocks and talked about what they had, they all were involved. Also, they got to hear other ways of thinking and were learning from one another.

"See," I overheard Nick saying to Shaney after she rolled an eleven, "you don't have to count all those out. Just take one long and one unit. That's eleven."

"Okay," she said. I'm not sure that Shaney truly understood that maneuver at the time, but I know that with time and experience she will. Her interaction with Nick will help her. And in the process, Nick's explanation helps him to cement his understanding. It seems to me that all students benefit from working in heterogeneous groups.

The children loved the game. It was wonderful to see them all so involved, animated, and learning.

REPRESENTING NUMBERS WITH BASE TEN BLOCKS

After the children were comfortable playing Race for a Flat, I introduced an activity with the Base Ten Blocks that would give me information about how the children connected the blocks to numbers. Each child had a place-value board, and there was a supply of blocks for each group to use.

I gave the first direction. "Put twenty-three on your board," I said, writing "23" on the chalkboard. As I circulated, I noticed that most children quickly put out two longs and three units. Several, however, counted out twenty-three units. One child, Jason, put out one long, and then added an additional thirteen units.

This was one of those situations in the classroom when I had asked a question for which I had one particular answer in mind—in this case, two longs and three units. Here I was presented with three different responses, all of which were correct. It reminded me that it's extremely important to be open to other ways children think about situations.

"I see three different ways to show twenty-three," I said to the class. "Laura did it the way I see on most of your boards. Tell what you have on your board, Laura, and I'll make a record of it on the chalkboard." Laura reported that she had two longs and three units. I drew a facsimile of the place-value board with two longs and three units on it.

"Bayard did it a different way," I said. "Tell what is on your board, Bayard, and I'll draw that." Bayard said he had twenty-three of the units, and I drew twenty-three small squares in the units column of a place-value board below the other. I drew them in rows of five, with one row of three, and pointed out to the children how organizing them like that makes counting easier than if I had drawn the squares in one big heap.

"Jason did it another way," I said then.

"I have one long," Jason reported. He stopped, counted his units, and concluded, "And I have thirteen units." I drew this option on the chalkboard.

"How is it possible that these three different answers each represents the number twenty-three?" I asked.

Children were eager to respond.

"Bayard did it with all ones, but Laura exchanged," Jill said.

"If you count Jason's," Erika said, "you get ten, eleven, twelve, thirteen, fourteen, all the way to twenty-three."

"Jason did some exchanging, but not all," Patrick reported.

After all the children who wanted to had spoken, I gave a similar problem. "This time," I said, "show 103 on your board." The children got busy, Some were interested in finding different ways. I asked that they show just one way on their boards.

I recorded all the suggestions they made, sometimes drawing the blocks and other times using numbers. For example, I drew the blocks for Grace's response of one flat and three units, and for Michael's answer of ten longs and three units. However, it was too cumbersome to draw suggestions such as Mairead's: seven longs and thirty-three units.

After this, I had the children return to playing Race for a Flat for the remainder of the period.

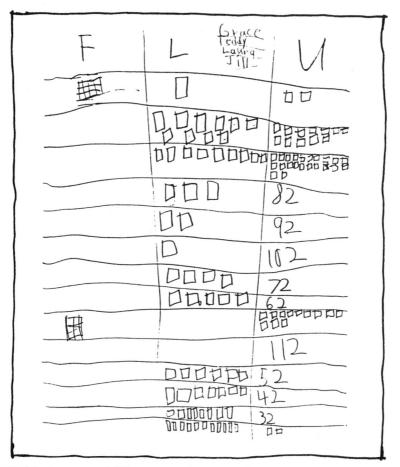

Grace, Teddy, Laura, and Jill use a combination of pictures and numerals to represent the different ways to show 112.

Tim, Michael, Michelle, and Alana write sentences to describe how to show 112 with the Base Ten Blocks.

How Many Different Ways

1. You can put down one flat, 1 long, and 2 units.
2. You can put down 112 units.
3. You can put down 1 flat and 12 units.
4. You can put down 10 longs and 12 units.
5. You can put down 9 longs and 22 units.
6. You can put down 8 longs and 32 units.
7. You can put down 7 longs and 42 units.
8. You can put down 11 longs and 2 units.
9. You can put down 4 longs and 62 units
10. You can put down 3 longs and 72 units.
11. You can put down 2 longs and 82 units.
12. You can put down 1 long and 92 units.
13. You can put down 6 longs and 52 units.
14. You can put down 5 longs and 62 units

HOW MANY DIFFERENT WAYS TO MAKE 112

The next day, I gave the children a problem to work on in their groups. Though this had not been on my original agenda for the Base Ten Blocks, I planned the problem in response to what had happened when the children found different ways to represent 23 and 103.

I explained the problem to the children. "I'd like you to find all the different ways you can to represent the number 112. Work together as a group, and record the ways you find on one paper." I had never tried this particular

Rather than display the different ways to represent 112, Kendra, Marina, and Bryce tell how many ways they found and describe the method they used.

How many ways

Kendra
Marina
Bryce

We found out that thear are forteen ways posable. We Know this becay6e we used up the only two ways to use a flat and No San that We used the ways with eleven longs, ten longs, nine longs, ect. We also used all units.

activity with children before. I was curious to see what they would do with the task—who would be able to find all the possible ways, how they would record their findings, and how they would work together on this task.

When they began work, several groups had questions. Patrick asked if it was all right for his group to make a chart. Brandie wanted to know if they could draw pictures. Michelle asked if they should write sentences. In each case, I told the group that they should choose a way to record that made sense to them, one they thought would make sense to others who read their paper.

The children worked on the problem for about forty minutes. All began their search randomly, but some groups looked for patterns after a while. Also, groups recorded their findings in different ways.

Four of the seven groups found all fourteen ways. Patrick, Vanessa, Ann, and Amber made a chart, entering the number of flats, longs, and units they used.

Grace, Teddy, Laura, and Jill also made a chart, recording with a combination of pictures of blocks and numbers. Grace made the chart while the others built possibilities on their boards.

Tim, Michael, Michelle, and Alana listed fourteen sentences: *"1. You can put down one flat, 1 long, and 2 units. 2. You can put down 112 units. 3. You can put down 1 flat and 12 units,"* and so on.

Kendra, Marina, and Bryce made a list of the ways they found, and then added an explanation at the end: *"We found out that thear are forteen ways posable. We know this because we used up the only two ways to use a flat and we saw that we used the ways with eleven longs, ten longs, nine longs, ect. We also used all units."*

The group with Tiare, Erika, Tara, and Andreas was satisfied after finding just one way each. Tiare made the record for the group while each of the others drew a picture of what they had built. When I asked them if there were other ways, they responded that they had built their favorite ways. This had taken them a good deal of time, and they were no longer interested in the pursuit.

Shaney, Nick, Mairead, and Gabe worked in a similar way, each finding a different way to make 112. They drew their own findings on the group paper. They did this twice, finding eight ways. They worked to find more, but were not successful.

Jason, Bayard, and Brandie found six ways. After talking about each one, they divided the work. Jason built each one with the blocks, Brandie drew pictures, and Bayard recorded. Their paper read: *"1. There are one flat and one long and two small bloks. 2. There is 11 longs and two small. That comes to 112. 3. We put one of the flats and 12 of the small bloks. 4. We put 90 longs and 23 small ones. 5. We put 50 longs and 62 small ones. 6. We put 112 small ones."*

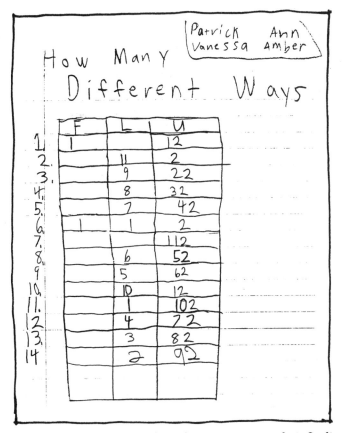

	F	L	U
1	1		12
2		11	2
3		9	22
4		8	32
5		7	42
6	1	1	2
7			112
8		6	52
9		5	62
10		10	12
11		1	102
12		4	72
13		3	82
14		2	92

How Many Different Ways

Patrick Ann
Vanessa Amber

Patrick, Vanessa, Ann, and Amber use a chart to organize their findings for representing 112 with Base Ten Blocks.

BASE TEN RIDDLES

To refocus them on exchanging, I presented riddles to the children the next day. I gave them clues, and they showed what they thought fit my clues by putting blocks on their place-value boards.

"For all these sets of clues," I told the children, "I've done all the exchanges possible. The first riddle is: I have four blocks worth 31." Most of the children were able to solve this riddle after a few moments. Grace presented her solution of three longs and one unit. I asked her to explain why the solution made sense.

"Because I used four blocks, and three longs make 30 and one more makes 31," she said. I drew her solution on the board.

I continued with other riddles of this same kind: "I have four blocks worth 13." "I have five blocks worth 32." I have four blocks worth 121." For each response, I had the child explain the solution and then drew it on the board. Soon, these riddles were simple for all the children.

"Can we have some harder ones, please?" Gabe asked in an exasperated tone.

"I'll try," I answered, and presented another riddle. "I have three blocks. Altogether, they are worth more than 200." There are three correct answers for this riddle. Some children found all, some found some, and some didn't find any. I continued with more riddles of this kind, until all the children were able to be successful: "I have two blocks worth less than 100." "I have two blocks worth more than 100, but less than 200." "I have three blocks worth less than 50."

Then I gave a third type of riddle: "I have four blocks that include three different sizes. They are worth less than 200." Adding the extra condition made this riddle more difficult for some of the children. I continued with more of this type: "I have five blocks worth less than 29. There are two different sizes of blocks." "I have six blocks that come in two different sizes. They are worth less than 50." For some of the children, this was too much information to deal with. I changed to another activity.

CLEAR THE BOARD

I then taught the children to play a game similar to Race for a Flat. In this game, each child starts with one flat, one long, and one unit. The dice tell them how many units to remove from their board.

As with the other game, I demonstrated this game for the class with one of the groups. I had Gabe, Mairead, Nick, and Shaney put one flat, one long, and one unit on each of their boards. I asked Nick to roll the dice. He rolled a seven.

"The seven tells you that you have to remove seven units from the board," I said.

"Can I exchange?" Nick asked.

"Yes," I answered. When Nick did so, he got confused in a way I've encountered before. He added enough units to his board so that he had ten altogether. In the shuffle, he incorporated the unit that was already there.

Children work cooperatively to find three Base Ten Blocks worth more than 200.

"How many units make a long, Nick?" I asked.

"Ten," he answered.

"How many units are on your board now?" I asked. Nick counted and reported that there were ten.

"Something's not right," I said, "because you started with one on the board and then got ten more, and now you have only ten altogether." Nick was confused.

"I'm going to ask you to do this again, Nick," I said, "because you've made a mistake that's easy to make. Start again with one of each block on the board." Nick did this.

"Now line up ten units against the long you're going to exchange." He did this.

"And now push those ten units over to the units column where the other unit is." Nick did this and counted the units.

"I have eleven," he said, and seemed satisfied.

"I think that's the best way to do exchanges so you avoid miscounting," I said. Nick then removed seven units and was left with four.

"Also," I added, "it's a good idea for everyone in the group to watch and help the others avoid mistakes."

I then had each of the other children take a turn. On her turn, Shaney rolled a twelve. This required that she exchange her flat for ten longs and then exchange two longs. If no one had rolled a twelve on the first roll, I would have continued the play so the children could see a flat being exchanged as well.

The children seemed to understand the rules and were eager to play. "There is one more rule you need to know about," I said. "You need to clear your board exactly. If there are seven units left, for example, and that's all, you can't win by rolling a sum larger than seven. Because of this, any time you want, you can choose to roll one die instead of two."

Michael had a question. "If you roll less than seven, can you take some off?" he asked.

"Yes," I replied. "That's okay. You just can't take off less than you roll on the dice."

"Could we play so if you roll too much you have to put some on instead?" Jill asked.

"That is another rule that we could use," I answered, "but for now, let's play the way I suggested."

The children spent what was left of the math period playing this game. Some got further than others in the game because some groups still were spending a great deal of their time organizing the blocks and negotiating the order of their turns. However, this beginning was much smoother than the one on the first day of playing Race for a Flat.

MORE IDEAS

I continued over time with Base Ten Block activities with the children. Sometimes I would try several "imagine" exercises. For those, I would have the children close their eyes while I told them what I'd like them to imagine.

"I'd like you to see three longs and three units on the board," I began. "Now imagine that you are putting four more units on the board. When you think you know how much you have on your board altogether, raise your hand."

I recorded their responses by writing the complete problem on the board: 33 + 4 = 37. For some children, this was easy and obvious; for others, it was new and still perplexing. With practice, however, all improved.

Soon I was giving them addition and subtraction problems, with and without regrouping. For example, I asked them to imagine two longs and eight units, and then to add four more units to their boards.

Jill gave the answer, and an explanation of what she had imagined. "I saw two longs and eight units," she said, "and then I saw my hand pushing four more units on the board. I put two with the eight and got a long, and then there were two units left. So I had three longs and two units."

Another problem I presented was to start with three longs and remove five units. "That's easy," Patrick said, "you do it just like playing Clear the Board. You end up with 25 left."

On one day, I gave the children a more difficult task. They struggled, somewhat bravely, but most were very confused. I had introduced the problem with a different kind of imagine exercise.

"Imagine you have four longs on your board," I said. "Now imagine what else you would need to add to your board so that you would have exactly one flat after you exchanged." This was easy for the children. Some knew that 40 and 60 make 100; others "saw" the blocks.

"What if you started with five longs and five units?" I asked. "What more do you have to add to get one flat when you exchange?" This was more difficult for them, so I had them use their blocks to figure it out. They muddled through.

After a few more of those, I gave each group the problem of figuring out how much more it would take to get two flats starting with three different numbers—55, 134, and 107. "Not only do I want your answer," I said, "I want you to explain how you got your answer." Four of the groups were able to solve the problems; three floundered.

Even with the difficulty some children experienced on this last task, all the children had become more facile with numbers from working with the Base Ten Blocks. They enjoyed the games, tackled the problems willingly, and became more comfortable talking and figuring with numbers. The Base Ten Blocks are a valuable manipulative for helping develop children's understanding of our system of place value.

PART

III

Geometry and Measurement Experiences

The geometry lessons traditionally included in primary textbooks focus children on learning to recognize shapes—squares, triangles, circles, rectangles. Textbook pages typically show a collection of shapes and ask children to identify all that match a given figure, making learning the proper names of shapes the main objective for primary children.

Measurement lessons for young children ask them to compare lengths, to explore area through covering shapes with squares, and to learn about standard units. The focus is on developing children's skill with measuring.

Though it is important for children to learn to recognize basic geometric shapes and to learn their names, and to become familiar with standard units of measurement, instruction that focuses on just these goals is not enough. In the area of geometry, children should have the opportunity to learn about the properties of geometric shapes, to compare shapes, to explore relationships among them, and to have concrete experiences with geometric principles. In learning about measurement, children need experiences in which they use measurement skills to explore mathematical concepts and solve problems.

The four chapters in this section suggest ways to present problem-solving activities to children that engage them with concepts in geometry, measurement, or both. In Chapter 9, first graders explore the different shapes that can be made from arranging four triangles. In Chapter 10, measurement problems using Cuisenaire Rods are presented to first and third graders, involving them with the concept of ratio. Chapter 11 describes a sequence of lessons done with a third-grade class in which they investigate a collection of containers in a variety of ways. In Chapter 12, third graders learn about symmetry from explorations with four toothpicks.

Geometry and measurement concepts are incorporated into other lessons in the book as well. In Chapter 1, children consider the amount of macaroni that will fill a jar after they make their necklaces, an experience in estimating volume. In Chapter 4, the experience of estimating scoops of beans also involves children with the measurement of volume. In Chapter 8, several of the place-value activities presented to children have them measure time, area, and volume.

Chapter 9
The Four-Triangle Problem

In this lesson with first graders, children explore shapes made from construction-paper triangles. The experience provides children with the opportunity to see shapes in relationship to each other and introduces them to the vocabulary and geometric concepts of diagonal, square, triangle, rectangle, parallelogram, trapezoid, pentagon, and hexagon. The lesson also provides children with experience in sorting and classifying shapes, helps to develop their spatial reasoning abilities, and encourages flexible thinking.

The initial lesson with the children took one class period that lasted just over an hour. However, the children continued to investigate the shapes they made for several weeks. Possibilities for extensions of this activity seem endless. This chapter offers just a beginning.

BEGINNING THE EXPLORATION

I began by giving each child a three-inch square of construction paper and a pair of scissors. "In a moment, you are going to fold and cut your square into two pieces," I said. "Watch carefully as I do mine, because I want you to do yours exactly the same way."

I showed them how to fold the square in half on the diagonal, open it, and cut along the diagonal to cut the square into two triangles. As I did this, I used the word *diagonal* so that the children would become familiar with it in the context of their activity. I also talked about the two resulting shapes. Most of the children knew they were called triangles. I wrote the words *square, diagonal,* and *triangle* on the chalkboard.

"Can you put your two triangles back together to make a square?" I asked. "Place them on your desk and see if you can do this." Some of the children were able to do it instantly. Others had to fiddle with the triangles a bit before making the square, but all were eventually successful.

"What I want you to do now," I said, "is to see if you can put your triangles together to make a different shape. But I want you to follow a rule. You must place your triangles so that two edges are touching, and those two edges have to be the same length." I showed them, using my triangles, what was allowed and what was not allowed.

"When you have a shape," I continued, "raise your hand so I can come and see what you've made."

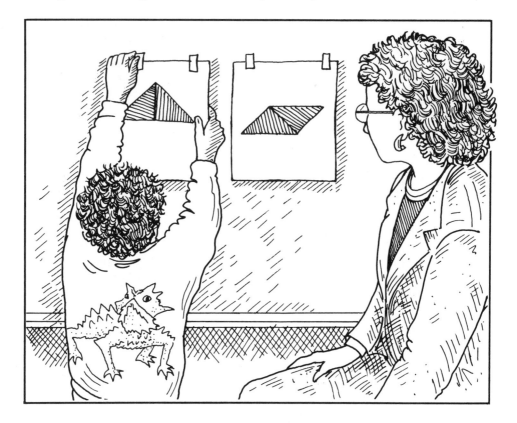

The children got busy. Melissa found a shape first, and raised her hand. She had put her two triangles together to make a parallelogram. I had her paste her parallelogram on a piece of 9-inch-by-12-inch newsprint and post it on the chalkboard.

Erick put his two triangles together to make a larger triangle. I asked him to paste his triangle on newsprint and post it next to Melissa's parallelogram.

I then called the class to attention. "Melissa and Erick have posted the shapes they made. Did anyone else get a shape like the one Melissa made?" Some of the children raised their hands. I took Melissa's shape off the chalkboard and rotated it into several other positions to help other children check to see if their shape was the same. Seeing whether they had the same shape was difficult for some of the children, especially if their shape was the flip of Melissa's.

"This shape has a name," I said. "It's called a parallelogram. Try to say parallelogram softly to yourself after me." I repeated the word several times for the children. Then I wrote it on the chalkboard under the other words.

"Now look at the shape Erick made," I said. "Who knows the name for this shape?" Several children raised their hands; others called out that it was a triangle.

I then reviewed with the children what they had done so far. I had the children respond to a series of questions. "What shape did you each start with?" "Who remembers the name of the line you got when you folded your square?" "What did you have when you cut your square?" "What other shapes did we make from the two triangles?"

EXPLAINING THE PARTNER ACTIVITY

"Now I'm going to have you work with a partner," I went on. "You'll each have a square to start with. One of you will have a green square; the other will have a purple square. First, cut your square in half on the diagonal, just as you did before. What pieces will you have?" They all knew they would have two triangles.

"How many triangles will you and your partner have altogether?" I asked. Most of the children knew that they would have four.

"This time," I continued, "you and your partner will take all four of your triangles and put them together to make another shape. You'll have to follow the same rule that you did before. Who can tell what the rule is?"

"They have to touch," Tina said.

"Yes, that's right," I said, "but there's something else to remember about the sides that touch."

Richmond raised his hand. "The sides have to be even," he said.

Ari had another way to say that. "They have to fit exactly," he said.

I then restated the rule for them. "When you put your triangles together, the sides must touch, and the sides that touch must be the same length."

I then continued with the directions. "When you have a shape that you're both satisfied with," I explained, "raise your hands so I can check that it follows the rule. Then take a piece of newsprint from the supply table and paste your shape on it as Melissa and Erick did. When you've done that, write your names on the newsprint." I reviewed the directions once more, and the children then got busy.

All but two of the pairs of children arranged their triangles into a rectangle. One pair made a square from the four triangles. Another pair made a triangle.

When all had finished the task, I had each pair of children come and post their shapes on the chalkboard. I had them post the shapes in three rows, one for the rectangles, one for the square, and one for the triangle, thus organizing their shapes into a graph. There were nine rectangles, one square, and one triangle.

I asked the children questions, as I would about any graph. "Which shape appears most often?" "How many rectangles are posted?" "How many triangles?" "How many squares?" "How many shapes are posted altogether?" "How many shapes posted are not rectangles?"

Annie raised her hand. "The rectangles aren't all the same," she said.

"What do you mean?" I asked.

"See the one that is a green square next to a purple square?" Annie explained. "The others are different."

"That's interesting for us to examine more closely," I said. "How many different kinds of rectangles are posted? Talk about this with your partner, and then I'll ask what you think."

While the children discussed this subject between themselves, I checked what was posted. There were five variations, three with duplicates. I was curious to hear how the children would describe the differences among the rectangles. I called the class to attention.

"Annie described one rectangle as a green square next to a purple square," I said. "How many like that do you see?" There were three of them, and the children pointed them out easily.

"Who can describe a different rectangle?" I asked.

I called on Aaron. "There's one with a green triangle in the middle and a purple triangle on each side."

"Can you find that one?" I asked the class. "Which one is it?"

"It's that one!" Hassan called out excitedly.

"Which one, Hassan?" I asked. "Is it the first one?" I pointed to the first rectangle in the row. "The second one? The third?" In this way, I reinforced the ordinal numbers, important for the first graders to learn. The rectangle Aaron described was the fifth one in the row.

"Can someone describe a different rectangle?" I went on.

I had Derek answer. "There's one that goes green, purple, green, purple."

There were several responses. "Oh, yeah." "That's the one we were going to say." "Let's see, it's the fourth one." "There's another, the next to the last."

I continued this procedure for the others. The children were animated and stayed interested.

Finally, I said, "I'll bet there are other color arrangements of rectangles that could be made. In a moment, I'm going to give you and your partner more squares so you can investigate not only other ways to make rectangles, but also other color arrangements for the square and the triangle that are also posted.

"Also," I continued, "I know another way you and your partner could have arranged your four triangles." I pasted two green and two purple triangles into a hexagon, a shape that was not a familiar one for the children.

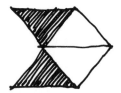

"Did I follow the rule of having sides the same length touching?" I asked. The children agreed that I did.

"If I were going to add mine to our graph, where would I put it?" I asked. Jennifer responded, "You'd have to start another row." I agreed with her.

"What do you call it?" Richard asked.

"It looks like an arrow," Carmen said.

"Let's see how many sides it has," I said. I counted the sides, marking each with an X. There were six Xs. "A shape with six sides is called a hexagon," I said, adding that name to the chalkboard list. I introduced the hexagon because I was going to have the children make additional shapes, and I wanted to suggest that others also were possible.

EXTENDING THE PARTNER ACTIVITY

Then, half an hour into the lesson, I gave the children directions so they could continue exploring shapes with their partners.

"I'm interested in seeing how many other shapes you can find," I explained. "You may find new shapes, such as I did with the hexagon. Or you may find different color arrangements for shapes you've already made. Either sort of variation is okay as long as you follow the rule about matching sides."

I then reinforced that I wanted them to work together on this activity. "You and your partner are to work together," I said. "Each time you find a shape that you agree is different from what you've already made, paste it on a piece of newsprint. Then get two more squares and try to find another. Keep the shapes you make in a pile. Are there any questions?"

There were none, and the children were eager to get to work. I put a stack of green and purple squares at each table along with a stack of newsprint. The children got busy, and worked for another thirty-five minutes.

Some of the partners worked more quickly than others. Muhran and Derek made the fewest number of shapes; they completed three. Derek did most of the work, as it was difficult for Muhran. But Muhran was able to contribute, mostly by printing his and Derek's names carefully on each paper. Mark and Nancy completed the greatest number of shapes, making ten.

Some of the children made shapes that were the same as others they had already made, not checking carefully through their pile. Still, there was a rich variety after the work time, providing much material for future sorting activities.

FURTHER EXPLORATIONS

I collected all the children's shapes into one pile, including the ones I had previously posted. On another day, I divided the shapes so each group had a stack. "First, cut each of the shapes out of the newsprint," I said. I cut out one shape to demonstrate. I wanted the children to cut the shapes so they could more easily compare them to one another.

The children work with partners to make different shapes from four triangles.

"When you've done that," I continued, "sort your stack into four piles. Make a pile of squares, one of rectangles, one of triangles, and a pile of all the other shapes.

After collecting the sorted shapes, I said, "What I'd like to do now is find all the different arrangements of rectangles that you made."

I took a rectangle from the pile and posted it. Then I held up another rectangle and asked, "Is it the same or is it different from the one I've already posted?" The children saw that it was different, so I posted it beside the first one.

I continued through the pile of rectangles, holding up each one for the children to examine and decide whether it was the same or different. I added one criterion. "If I turn a rectangle upside down," I said, "and it looks the same as one that is already posted, then it doesn't count as a different arrangement."

The children were excited about this activity. Some began to shout out their thoughts. To calm them down, I asked that children indicate with thumbs up or thumbs down whether they thought the rectangle I was showing was different or not. That helped.

Discerning differences was easier for some children than for others. Some needed to touch the rectangles as they described the arrangement. "See, it goes green, purple, purple, green, just like that one," Michael said, coming up and pointing to the arrangements. Other children started to think about arrangements that were missing from the chart. "We need a purple, green, purple, green, with the lines going the other way," Melissa said, using her hands to explain what she meant. We went through all the rectangles they had made.

The next day, I repeated this investigation for the triangles and squares they had made, posting them into a separate row for each. I then made a suggestion. "If you think of other arrangements of rectangles, triangles, or squares that aren't posted, make them. Then the class will check to see if they agree that they should be posted."

On another day, we sorted the rest of their shapes. Those left were four-sided shapes other than squares or rectangles, and some five- and six-sided shapes. As I had done before, I distributed some of these to each group. "Work together," I said, "and sort your shapes according to the number of sides they have." I demonstrated counting the sides of several shapes for the children, modeling for them how to keep track of the sides as they counted. I posted their shapes.

By now, the entire chalkboard on the side of the room was filled with shapes made from the green and purple triangles. The display kept children's interest for a period of several weeks. They found new arrangements and new shapes. They continued to talk about the shapes, and often went over to look at something more closely or to point out something to a classmate. The activity was a rich one for the children.

A CHALLENGE FOR OLDER STUDENTS AND ADULTS

How many different shapes can be made from the four triangles? And how many different color variations?

Chapter 10
Exploring Ratio

Ratio and proportion are concepts that are usually thought to be complicated and difficult for students. Most adults remember their own experiences with ratio and proportion as confusing, requiring setting up a problem according to "this is to this as that is to that" and then applying some sort of rule to solve it, such as cross-multiplying. Usually, the focus of such experiences was the mechanics of working with the numbers, rather than thinking about a problem-solving situation.

It is unusual for children in the primary grades to learn about ratio and proportion. When students are first introduced to these concepts, often in the middle of junior high school math class, they have no base of experience on which to build. Also, the time needed to develop understanding is too often not available, and the students are prematurely plunged into finding solutions for problems.

This chapter describes two lessons, one with a class of first graders and another with third graders. Both lessons use Cuisenaire Rods to present problems for children to solve. The lessons were meant to enhance children's understanding of number, provide them with an experience in measuring, while giving them an opportunity to use the ideas of ratio and proportion.

A LESSON WITH FIRST GRADERS

The children had had previous experiences over time with the Cuisenaire Rods. They had had many opportunities to explore freely with the rods, during which they built many structures—houses, roads, trucks, people, starbursts, and staircases. The children had also been introduced to several activities with the rods. They had learned to play a guessing game that helped them become more familiar with the colors of the different lengths of rods. They had engaged in making trains of rods equal in length to other rods. They had used the rods for measuring and comparing.

Though the children always enjoyed the chance to build with the rods, they were also willing to interrupt their own explorations and focus on activities I suggested. On this day, I did not distribute the rods to the children. Instead, I asked them to make a measurement estimate.

"How many orange rods do you think it would take to measure across the classroom puppet stage?" I asked the class.

Guesses varied, with most in the ten to twenty range. I then used the rods to measure, while the children counted. The puppet stage was just about nine orange rods long.

I then posed a problem for the children to work on in pairs. "You and your partner are to figure out how many yellow rods it would take to measure across the stage," I said. "To help you think about this problem, I'll give you each one yellow and one orange rod. The two of you have to agree on one answer and then record your answer, writing why you think it is correct."

Partners immediately got involved in discussions. When circulating, I heard different approaches. "I think it would be a lot, maybe twenty or thirty." "But we have to agree on one answer." "See, it takes two of the yellows to make one orange." "I think we add nine and nine." One pair of children, Julie and Richard, went to the puppet stage with a yellow rod and estimated, moving it across the stage and counting.

Though about half of the children arrived at the answer of eighteen, only Jenny and Jason were able to relate the orange and yellow rods in their explanation. Jenny read what they wrote: *We think that it is 18 because 9 + 9 = 18 and 2 yellows make an orange.*

Others explained in a variety of ways. Ryan and Kelly, for example, wrote: *becuse we counted the blocks alot.*

Jenny reads the explanation she and Jason wrote about why eighteen yellow rods are needed to measure the puppet stage.

Marigrace and Amin had a different explanation. They wrote: *"It is 18 because 9 + 9 = 18. 18 is the best number. It is the best number we had."*

Jennifer and Darryl wrote a similar explanation for the answer of twenty: *"We think its going to be 20. 10 + 10 = 20."*

After the children had reported their answers, I again measured across the puppet stage, this time using yellow rods. The children counted to eighteen as I laid the yellow rods end to end.

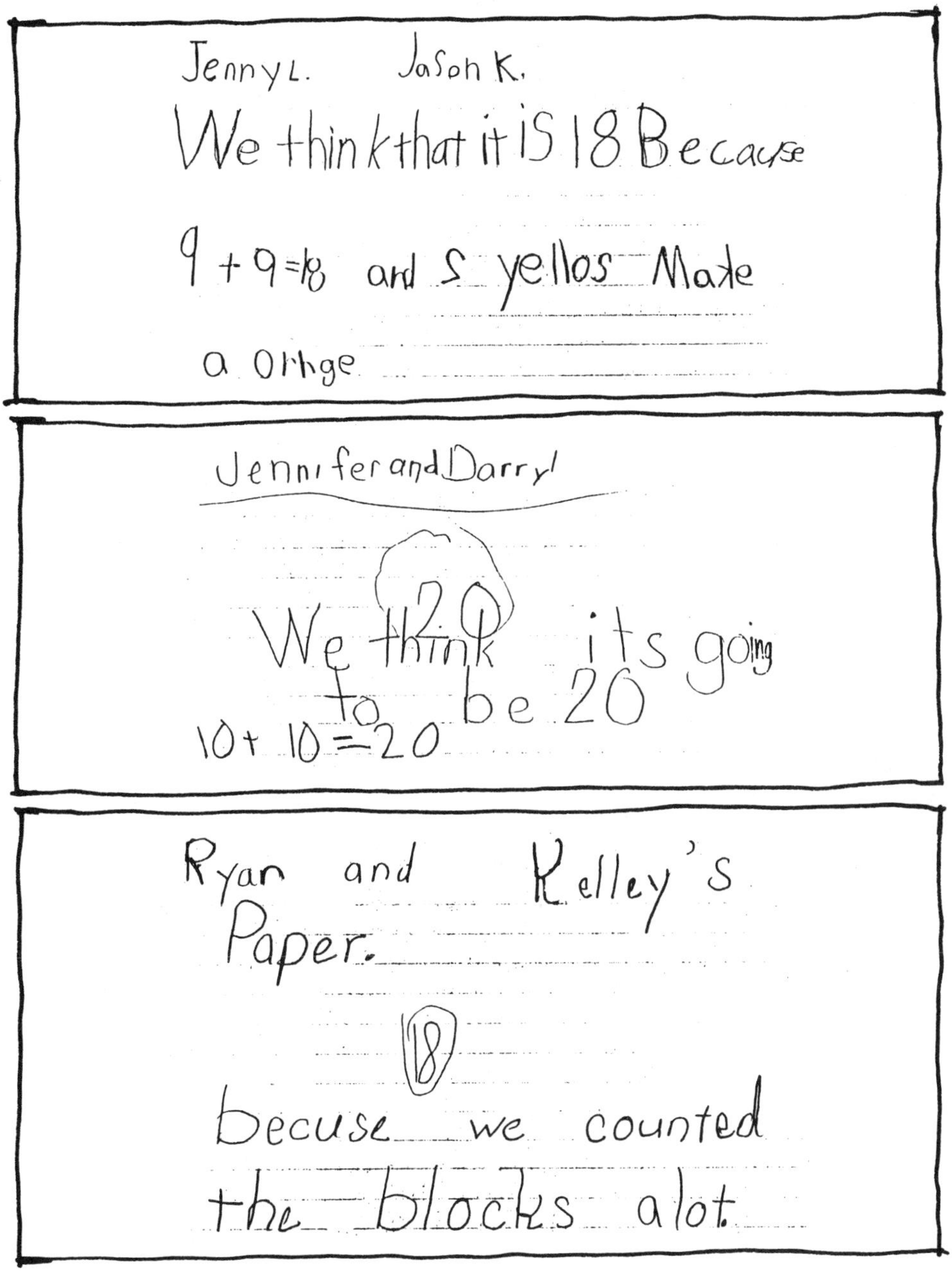

Jenny L.   Jason K.

We think that it is 18 Because

9 + 9 = 18   and 2 yellos Make

a Orhge

Jennifer and Darryl

We think its going to be 20

10 + 10 = 20

Ryan and Kelley's Paper.

18

becuse we counted the blocks alot

The children describe how many yellow Cuisenaire Rods are needed to measure the puppet stage that is nine orange rods long.

I presented a similar challenge to a class of third graders, extending the problem to include rods of other colors as well. To begin the lesson, I asked each pair of children to take one rod of each color and put the rest away.

"Look around the room," I said to the class, "and see if there is something that you think is just about twelve orange rods long."

Sean raised his hand. "I think the sentence strip on the board," he said. He was referring to a sentence the children used for handwriting practice. I measured it; it took eight rods.

Irene had another suggestion. "Across my desk," she said. I laid orange rods end to end across her desk. Eleven rods fit, with some extra room, but not enough for another rod.

"I'm looking for something that is just about twelve orange rods long," I said. "What else can we try?"

"That bulletin board," Joshua suggested, pointing to the small bulletin board by the door. I measured, moving one orange rod across while the children counted. It was just short of thirteen orange rods.

"What about the bookshelf?" Emily asked. It was ideal. Twelve rods fit across it with less than half a centimeter to spare.

"Now that we have something that is just about twelve orange rods long," I said, "talk with your partner about how many yellow rods it will take to measure the bookshelf. In a few minutes, you'll have a chance to tell your answer. Also, be prepared to explain how you arrived at that answer."

This was easy for the children to do, and they were ready to report quickly. Rebecca reported for herself and Tomo. "Two yellow fit on one orange," she said, "so we did two times twelve and got twenty-four."

Edward reported next for himself and Eileen. "We did it sort of the same," he said. "We did twelve times two, twelve orange times two, and we got twenty-four."

Mark raised his hand to report for himself and Irene. "There are twelve orange and two yellow make an orange, so we counted by twos," he explained. "We think the answer is twenty-four too."

Jessica and Brian used a different method. Jessica reported: "We knew that two yellow make an orange. We only had one yellow, so we made another yellow with a magenta and a tan. Then we'd need twelve yellow rods and twelve of the magenta and tan. We added twelve and twelve together and got twenty-four."

"Do we need to check your answer by measuring?" I asked. I was answered with a chorus of yeses. Even though the children were confident about their reasoning, they still felt the need for verification with the concrete material. I measured across the bookshelf to prove that it took twenty-four yellow rods.

"I'd like you to try the same problem for other rods," I told the children. "Work in pairs, but feel free to talk as a group of four if you think that will help. First, figure out how many red rods will fit across the bookshelf. Then try dark green and, if you have time, any other color you would like. Record your answers and write explanations of your reasoning."

The children got to work. All pairs figured that it would take sixty red rods to measure the bookshelf, based on the relationship that it takes five red rods to make one orange. They reported different reasons, however.

Several pairs of children counted by fives. Sean and Josephine, for example, wrote: *"We think it will be 60 red rods long. We think this because there are five red rods in an orange rod. So we counted by fives 12 times and we got 60."*

Some used multiplication. Kristen and Shane recorded: *"We think it will be 60 red rods long. We think this because we measured five red rods on the orange and multiplyed 5 × 12."*

Some added. From Michael and Michelle: *"We think it takes 60 red rods to go across the shelf because 5 red rods make 1 orange and it takes 12 oranges to go across the shelf so we added 12 5 times."*

Finding how many dark green rods, however, was more difficult for most of the children. Some asked if they could use more rods. When I was asked, I

> We think it will be 60 red rods long.
> We think this because we measured five red rods on the orange and multiplyed 5 x 12.

> We think it takes 60 red rods to go across the shelf because 5 red rods make 1 orange and it takes 12 oranges to go across the shelf so we added 12 5 times.

> We think it will be 60 red rods long. We think this because there are five red rods in an orange rod. So we counted by fives 12 times and we got 60.

Third graders describe in different ways why it takes sixty red rods to measure the bookshelf that is twelve orange rods long.

We think it will 2 0 green rods long.

We think this because we put 3 orange rods in a row and we put 3 more rows of 3 on the botom. We fit 5 greens on top of all the 3 oranges and counted all the greens.

We think it takes 24 green rods because we meshurd our fingers and we did it across the desk and we rounded it off again.

We think it will be 20 green rods long. We think this because 3 orange eqaul 5 green and then we added five four times.

Figuring how many dark green rods are needed to measure the bookshelf poses a challenge for the students.

said it was okay, but that I was interested in having them think of some other way of doing it than just measuring across with the rods.

Some children used their desks as a reference, as the desks measured just under twelve orange rods. Mark and Irene reported, for example: *"We think it will be 20 dark green rods long. We think this because we mesured our desk by moving the green block along."*

Paul and Shauna reported: *"We think it takes 24 green rods because we meshurd our fingers and we did it across the desk and we rounded it off again."*

Rebecca and Tomo compared the orange and green rods. They wrote: *"We think it will be 20 green rods. We think this because 6 oranges make 10 dark greens and 10 + 10 = 20."*

Others also compared the two rods. Edward and Eileen wrote: *"We think it will be 20 green rods long. We think this because we put 3 orange rods in a row and we put 3 more rows of 3 on the botom. We fit 5 greens on top of all the 3 oranges and counted all the greens."* They made a drawing of what they had done.

Steve and Lee had a more abstract explanation. *"We think it will be 20 green rods long. We think this because 3 orange eqaul 5 green and then we added five four times."*

DEALING WITH CHILDREN'S CONFUSION

The children worked for about forty minutes on these problems. During that time, conversation was intense and involvement high. There were times when children were perplexed or confused, but most were not troubled by this. In these instances, I didn't interfere. Periods of confusion are a natural part of the learning process.

For some children, however, their frustration was interfering with their interest in the investigation. Lisa and James, for example, had correctly found the answer of sixty red rods by counting by fives. To solve the problem with dark green rods, however, they decided to count by threes, erroneously arriving at thirty-six. This disturbed them because several pairs of children around them had arrived at the answer of twenty. They called me over for help.

I asked some questions so I could understand their thinking. "Why did you count by fives to get the answer of sixty for the red rods?" I asked.

"Because five reds make an orange," James responded quickly. Lisa nodded her agreement.

"I agree that five red make an orange," I said. "How did that information help you get sixty?"

"Because there are twelve oranges," Lisa explained, "so you go five, ten, fifteen, twenty." She continued counting by fives, using her fingers to keep track of doing this twelve times.

"Why did you count by threes for the dark green rod?" I asked.

Neither had an immediate answer. They began to fiddle with the rods, comparing the dark green and orange rods.

Lisa and James are confused and need extra help.

"It takes three red rods to make a dark green," James finally said, having matched a train of three reds to a dark green rod.

"How does that information help you compare the dark green rods to the orange rods?" I asked.

Neither was able to find a reason for this or to explain why they counted by threes. They were getting into more of a muddle in their thinking.

I do not believe that telling or explaining is a useful teaching choice for developing children's understanding. Children need to make sense out of situations for themselves. I could have asked another pair of children who had arrived at twenty to explain how they did it, but it seemed to me this would merely be another version of telling.

To keep the emphasis on their thinking, I posed a new problem for them. "Try the white rod instead," I suggested. I chose this rod because ten white are equal to one orange, and I knew that their method of counting by fives and threes would translate to this situation. I was interested to see how they would solve this problem.

"Call me over when you've solved it," I said, and left them to work.

Lisa and James immediately got engaged with the new problem. After a while, they had written: *"We think it will be 120 white rods long. We think this because we counted by tens."* They called me over.

"Why did you count by tens?" I asked.

They were clear about this. "It takes ten whites to make an orange," Lisa said.

I suggested they try the blue rod next. The blue rod is closest in length to the orange rod; it is equal to nine white rods. I was interested in seeing how

> Lisa
> James
>
> ① We think it will be 60 red rods long. We think this because we counted by fives.
>
> 2. We think it will be 38 dark green roads long. We counted by threes.
>
> 3. We think it will be 120 white rods long.
>
> We think this because we counted by tens.
>
> 4. We think it will be 14 blue roads long We think this because we counted. ~~by 2~~ The blue road almost fits on the ornge road and the extra spaces will make 2 more blue roads.
>
> 5. We think it will be 32 light green rods long. We think this because we counted by threes.

Lisa and James's work is an indication of partially grasped ideas, a natural part of the learning process.

the children would deal with this problem. Their final answer was: *"We think it will be 14 blue roads long. We think this because we counted. The blue road almost fits on the ornge road and the extra spaces will make 2 more blue roads."* However, their written work showed a false start. They had written that they had *"counted by 2s,"* but later they had crossed this out.

Lisa and James then decided to try the light green rod. They got an answer of thirty-two. *"We think this because we counted by threes,"* they wrote. Though that wasn't correct, I didn't probe their thinking. Rather than judging the children's work as incorrect and trying to lead them to the correct conclusion, I accepted their work as an indication of partially grasped ideas, also a natural part of the process of developing understanding.

With other pairs of children, I responded similarly. Because more children seemed to have success with the white and blue rods, in retrospect, I think that it might have been better to assign the class the red, white, and blue rods to figure, with the dark green rod as an extra challenge.

Even though the problem was a struggle for the students, the thinking they did, their discussions about number relationships, and their experiences with explaining their reasoning made the time spent well worthwhile.

Chapter 11
Box Sorting

In this sequence of lessons, a class of third graders was involved with a wide range of experiences through investigating containers. The children compared containers and reported their similarities and differences; they sorted them by the different attributes; they identified the attributes by which others sorted their boxes; they solved the problem of covering all faces of their boxes with construction paper; they wrote descriptions that could be used to identify one specific box.

In preparation for this sequence of lessons, I asked each child to bring an empty box or container to school. The children brought a wide assortment—boxes from toothpaste, cereal, fruit rolls, jewelry, shoes, paper clips, oatmeal, and biscuits. Many brought two or three containers. Also, I brought about fifteen boxes to have on hand to supplement the class collection.

COMPARING BOXES

For the first lesson, I organized the children into pairs. "You each need one box," I told them. "You may use the one you brought, or you may choose a box from the ones I've brought." Most of the children decided to use a box they had brought. When all the children had boxes, I continued with instructions.

"First, you are to take turns and tell each other about the box you have, describing it in as many ways as you can. Then discuss together how your two boxes are the same and how they are different."

The children had much to say to one another, and their discussions were quite lively. I interrupted the class after a while to give an additional instruction.

"What I would like you to do now," I explained, "is to write down some of the things you noticed about how your boxes are the same and how they are different. I'd like you and your partner to report this on one piece of paper." I then showed on the chalkboard how I wanted them to organize their recording.

The children had no difficulty with this task. However, the writing took them quite a while. The children were learning to write in cursive, and took special care with forming letters. I let the children work for about fifteen minutes—long enough for each pair to have recorded several similarities and several differences.

"I'm going to have you report some of your findings," I told the class after calling them back to attention. "You and your partner will come up to the front of the room. One of you will show the two boxes you compared, while

Evan Leong
Kristen Chew

How are your boxs the same?
They both have 6 sides.
They both open one way.
They can both carry something.
How are yours boxs difrent?
One is a rectagle and one is a
sgause.
One of the boxs come a part and the
other does not.
One is bigger than the othes.

Michelle Shane

How our boxs are the same.
Because there both rectangles
They both are white.
They both can carry stuff.
They both have 4 sides.
They both can stand up.
They both can lay down.
They both can open up.
They both are empty.
How our boxs are diffrent.
One has a kid.
One's fatter.
One's bigger.
One's shthiner.
One's longer.
One flips better.
One has a stamp on it
One's darker.
One is whiter.

Partners record how their boxes are the same and how they are different.

the other will read one thing that is the same about your boxes and one thing that is different. Before we get started, decide who will do the reading and who will do the showing."

I think that taking the time for this reporting is important for several reasons. First of all, it acknowledges the work the children have done by asking them to share it publicly. Second, children get experience speaking in front of a group. Third, the children have the opportunity to hear what ideas others had and what language they used to describe their ideas.

The children reported their ideas seriously. Somehow, it felt like an important event in the class. This attitude might have been strengthened by the fact that it was the day they were having their class pictures taken, so some of the children were in their good clothes. Eddie was wearing a white shirt and tie!

Kim read while Brian showed the boxes: *"Both of our boxes have six sides. They are not the same size."*

Lee reported for himself and Lisa: *"They both are cardboard. One came with something to eat."*

Kristen read and Paul showed the boxes: *"Both boxes once had something in them. One box is taller than the other box."*

From Rebecca and Brandon: *"They both stand up. One is narrow and one is fat."*

From Steve and Shauna: *"They're both flat on the bottom. The boxes are not the same size."*

Tomo read for himself and Tracie: *"They both can open. Tracie's box is big and my box is small."*

Emily reported the similarity she had written for herself and Marc: *"Each of our boxes are rectangle and both of our boxes have corners."* Marc read the difference he had recorded: *"My box is bigger than hers."*

SORTING INTO TWO SETS

In a second lesson, the children worked in groups of four. Each group was instructed to take two additional boxes from the supply of extras to add to the four boxes they already had. Together, they were to explore ways to sort their six boxes into two groups and record how they did so.

I introduced this activity to the children by sorting six of the extra containers I had brought. I put two cylindrical containers in one group—an oatmeal box and an orange juice container. I put four boxes with rectangular faces in another—boxes that had held paper clips, baking chocolate, checks, and a small gift.

"Who can tell how I sorted these boxes?" I asked. Many of the children raised their hands. I called on Rebecca.

"Those have a circle," she said, pointing to the cylindrical containers, "and the others don't."

"Does anyone have a different idea?" I asked. Rather than accept a response as the one right answer, I wanted all children who had ideas to verbalize them. The opportunity to tell what they are thinking is a valuable experience for the children. Also, it encourages the idea that there are different ways to look at and describe a situation.

Michelle, Philip, Benson, and Shauna list twelve ways to sort their group's boxes.

Michelle
Philip
Benson
Shauna

1. fat and lean
2. cardboard and not cardboard
3. food containers and not food
   containers
4. smelly and not smelly
5. round and rectangle
6. tall and small
7. red and not red
8. letters and no letters
9. dark colors and light colors
10. top comes off and top
    doesn't come off
11. made in New York and
    not made in New York
12. holds paper and doesn't
    hold paper

I called on Benson. "The one with four boxes all are rectangles." Though Benson's language was not precise, he was certain about what he thought.

Steve had another idea. "Those had food in it," he said, referring to the oatmeal and juice containers. "The others didn't."

"Yes they did," Kim contradicted. "That one had chocolate in it," she continued, pointing to one of the others.

"Oh, yeah," Steve conceded.

"Any other ideas?" I asked.

"Those have corners," Edward said, pointing to the rectangular containers, "and the others don't."

"Let me show you how to record the ways you've sorted these boxes," I said, writing on the chalkboard as I reviewed their ideas. "For Rebecca's idea, I could write 'has circular faces' and 'doesn't have circular faces.' That's not exactly how Rebecca said it, but it means the same thing. For Benson's idea, I could write 'has no rectangular faces' and 'has rectangular faces.' For Edward's, I could write 'has corners' and 'doesn't have corners.' "

In this way, I used the children's ideas, but introduced more precise language to describe them. I think it's best for children to learn language through contexts of usage, and I was trying to contribute to their learning in this way.

I then told the children that they were to sort their boxes in as many ways as they could, recording each way they did so. The children got engaged immediately with this activity and worked on it for the remainer of the period. The groups listed from six to twelve different ways to sort their boxes. Some were ways I hadn't anticipated.

Kristen, Jim, Josephine, and Joshua, for example, recorded nine different ways to sort their boxes. They wrote: *"We sorted our boxes into these groups: 1. tall and short 2. thin and thick 3. big and small 4. light and hevvy 5. smells good and don't smell good 6. see through and not see through 7. made in USA and not made in USA 8. with plastic and without plastic 9. writing on it and no writing on it."*

A GUESSING GAME

I extended the activity from the second lesson into a third experience. In the third lesson, I planned to have each group show one way they had sorted their boxes and have the others guess how they had labeled the sets.

To introduce this lesson, I used the same six containers I had used for the previous lesson. I made two labels on strips of tag—"has circular faces" and "doesn't have circular faces"—and cut extra label cards so each group would have two. I also placed yarn on the rug in two large loops.

The children sat in a circle around the yarn loops. As they watched, I put the oatmeal box and the orange juice can in one loop and the remaining boxes in the other. I placed the labels describing each set on the correct loops, with the writing side turned face down.

"On the other side of the labels, I've written how I sorted these boxes," I told the children. "I'd like you to guess what they say."

I called on Philip first. "Round and rectangle," he said.

"Your idea is close," I said, "but those are not my words. I wonder if you can guess what I wrote."

Emily guessed next. "Cylinder and not cylinder."

"Still not my words," I said.

"Cardboard and not cardboard," Joshua offered.

"Tops come off on all and tops don't come off on all," Tom said.

"Round and not round," Josephine said.

When all the children who wanted to had guessed, I turned over my labels. "Lots of you had the same idea as I had," I said, "but you didn't use my words. Who can tell what I mean by 'circular faces'?"

Rebecca answered. "It means they have sides that are circles," she said.

"What kinds of faces do the other boxes have?" I asked.

"Rectangle," Tom answered.

"The other boxes have rectangular faces," I said, repeating Tom's idea, with the correct language.

Philip guesses how the boxes in the two loops are sorted.

Then I told the groups what their task was. "I am going to return your papers describing how you sorted your boxes. As a group, choose one way you sorted your boxes, and make label cards for it. Then we'll come back to the circle, and groups will take turns sorting their boxes and placing their labels for the others to guess."

Lee had a question. "Can we make up a new way?"

"No," I responded, "choose one that you have already found." I didn't want the children to take too much time for this, so I restricted them to the thinking they had already done. The children went back to their desks to prepare their labels.

When I gathered the children back on the rug, I explained how we would proceed. "When it is your group's turn," I said, "all of you come up to the front. Put the containers in the yarn loops and place your labels face down. Then you have two jobs. One is to call on people who want to guess. You'll take turns in your group doing that. The second job is to respond to the guesses. You can say 'Yes' or 'No' or 'Close, but we said it a different way.' "

Kristen, Jim, Josephine, and Joshua went first. In one loop, they put a coffee can and a box that had contained birdfeed. In the others, they had two toothpaste boxes, a flat gift box, and a box that had held envelopes.

The other children made lots of guesses, with no success—tall and short, big and little, many colors and just one color, has blue on it and doesn't have blue on it. Finally, the class was stumped, and so was I!

I asked for a hint. I took the baking chocolate box from the ones I had sorted and asked in which loop it should go. The group conferred with each other in whispers. "We can't tell," Kristen said.

"Oh," I replied, "you mean it's something you can't tell just by looking." They nodded yes.

The children now made new guesses.

"Crumbs inside and no crumbs inside," Marc suggested.

"Those are gray inside and those aren't," Jessica said.

None of the children's guesses was right.

"Give up?" the group asked. We admitted defeat, and they turned over their labels—"smelly" and "not smelly." We passed the boxes around to verify that there still was a hint of coffee and birdseed in those two containers. Kristen, Jim, Josephine, and Joshua were as pleased as could be.

We had time for one more group that day. Kelly, Lee, Tomo, and Tom placed their boxes. The first guess was a close one.

"Those hold food and those don't hold food," Emily said.

Kelly responded, "That's close, but we said it differently."

"Used to have something you can eat and didn't use to have something you can eat," Joshua said.

Lee responded, "That's not it."

Tomo gave a hint. "We used a hard word," he said.

The class was stumped. "Can we give another hint?" Kelly asked.

I said that was okay, but that they should talk about it as a group first. They went into a huddle and came out with a hint. "It starts with an *e*," Tomo said.

The children forgot the former hints, and concentrated solely on "e" words.

"Empty and not empty."

"Excellent and not excellent."

"Enormous and not enormous."

Finally, Michelle hit on it. "Edible and not edible," she said. The group turned over the labels. They had written *"Edable"* and *"Not edable."*

There was no more time that day, but we did a few each on the following three days so each group had its turn. The groups had used an assortment of labels—*"all cardboard"* and *"not all cardboard," "comes apart"* and *"doesn't come apart"* (they were talking about the lids), *"has writing on it"* and *"doesn't have writing on it," "has lids"* and *"doesn't have lids," "made in NY"* and *"not made in NY."* For this last one, the group gave a clue. "It was made somewhere," Michelle said.

After the last group had its turn, I asked the class what they thought they had learned from this activity. Their ideas mirrored mine.

"You learn what other people are thinking," Rebecca said.

"You learn new words," Kristen said.

"You learn about shapes," Brian said.

TRACING FACES

In the next lesson, I wanted the children to focus specifically on the faces of containers. I used the box that had contained checks to demonstrate to the children what they were to do.

"For this activity," I explained to the children, "your group of four needs to choose just one box from your collection. Your job is to trace the faces of the box you choose onto a piece of newsprint." I had 12-inch-by-18-inch newsprint for them to use for this.

"Watch as I trace my box," I continued. I began to work.

"How many faces do I have to trace?" I asked. I heard mostly the answer of "six"; some children answered "four."

When I had finished tracing the faces, I asked the children, "How can I be sure I have traced all the faces?" They had several suggestions. "You could count to make sure." "You could mark them when you're done." "You could match it and check."

"You will need to be sure that you've traced each of the faces of the box you pick," I said. "Also, I'd like you to plan ahead so you use just one sheet of paper to trace all the faces. If you'd like another sheet, you'll have to prove to me that one sheet was not enough." I stopped for questions. There were none.

"When you've completed your tracing, place the box you used on the counter and post your paper above it," I said. "Then we can see if we can tell which boxes match what is posted."

The children worked together well on this activity. All but one group was able to trace all faces on just one piece of paper. When the papers were posted, many children were interested in seeing which boxes matched which papers.

COVERING THE BOXES

The next task I planned for the children was for them to cover each of the group's six boxes with construction paper. Accomplishing this would involve them with the shapes and sizes of the faces of each container. Also, when the children covered the boxes, many of the attributes they had used to describe and sort their boxes would no longer be visible. I planned to take advantage of this fact and have them focus on the geometric attributes of the boxes, rather than on their former contents or on the lettering.

I demonstrated for the children what they were to do, again using the box that had held checks. I traced each face again, this time on construction paper. Then I cut them out and pasted them on the box.

The children got to work eagerly. In most groups, each child took a different box to cover, and those who finished first got to work on the remaining two.

It was interesting to watch the children work. It was difficult for some children to hold the box steady and trace around its faces. I think I would suggest from the outset that they work in pairs, with one child holding the

Emily, Kim, Paul, and Roger cover the faces of their boxes with construction paper.

box while the other traces. Some, but not many, traced a face and then doubled the paper, cutting two of them at once. Some had difficulty positioning the cut-out faces on the box and turned them this way and that. The cylindrical containers provided a challenge for all groups who had them.

It took a class period for all the boxes to be covered.

DESCRIBING ONE BOX

My next task for the children was for them to pick one of their group's boxes and describe it as many ways as they could. I introduced this task by choosing a box one group had covered. It was about the size of a shoe box.

"What can you tell me about this box?" I asked the children.

"It's tall," Tracie offered. I had rested the box on its small face. I changed its position so that it now rested on the long face.

"How about now?" I asked.

"Oooh, no," Tracie said, "it's not so tall now."

"I think it's big," Brian said.

"Is it big like a refrigerator box?" I asked.

"No, not so big," Brian answered.

"It's about a foot long," Philip said.

"Whose foot?" I asked. "A child's foot or an adult's foot?"

"A twelve-inch foot," Philip replied.

"Any other ideas?" I asked.

"The two main sides are large rectangles," Jessica said.

"What do you mean by 'the main sides'?" I asked her.

"I mean the big ones," she explained.

"Are you saying that the two large faces are rectangles?" I asked, prompting for correct terminology.

"Yes, that's what I meant," Jessica answered.

"It has eight corners," Sean said. I counted to verify for the class that this was so.

I then told the children what they were to do. "Your group is to choose one of your boxes to describe," I explained. "Write as many sentences as you can that tell something about your box. Be as specific as possible so that somebody who reads the sentences you write could identify the box you described."

"Do we each write sentences?" Kim asked.

"You may each write," I answered, "but work together as a group and put everyone's thoughts on one piece of paper."

"Can we use a ruler?" Philip asked.

"Yes, you may," I replied.

Philip's question seemed to influence the others, and most groups included measurements in their descriptions. For example, Philip, Michelle, Shauna, and Benson wrote:

1. *The biggest face is about 4 inches wide.*
2. *The biggest face is about 11-1/2 inches long.*
3. *The smallest face is about 4-1/2 inches long.*
4. *The smallest face is about 1-1/2 inches wide.*
5. *It can hold an envelope.*

Kristen, Marc, Tracie, and Sean wrote: *"It is much smaller than a refrigerator box. Our box has 8 corners. Our box has 6 faces. Our box top can come off. The longest side is 8 inches by 11 inches. The box is white inside. It is holow inside."*

From Paul, Emily, Kim, and Roger: *"I think the box that we choose is 8.5 inches long. This box is wider than a needle. But slimmer than a hand. This box is smaller than a ruler. Our box has four rectangle and two square faces."*

From Lee, Tomo, Tom, and Jessica:

1. *The bigest face is seven and three qauters long.*
2. *The bigest face is almost four inches wide.*
3. *The smallest face is four inches long.*
4. *The smallest face is two and one qauters wide.*
5. *Diagonally the biggest face is almost eight and a half inches wide.*

Lee Chretien Tomo Tom
Jessica Brennan

Box Description
1. The bigest face is seven and three gauters long.
2. The bigest face is almost fowr inches wide.
3. The smallest face is four inches long.
4. The smallest face is two and one gauters wide.
5. Diagonally the biggest face is almost eight and a half inches wide.

Michelle Philip Shauna
Benson

Box   Description
1. The biggest face is about 4 inches wide.
2. The biggest face is about 11½ inches long.
3. The smallest face is about 4½ inches long.
4. The smallest face is about 1½ inches wide.
5. It can hold an envelope.

Philip's request to use a ruler influences others to include measurements in their box descriptions.

Kristen C.
Marc
Tracie
Sean

Box Description

It is much smaller than a refrigerator box.

Our box has 8 corners.

Our box has 6 faces.

Our box top can come off.

The longest side is 8 inches by 11 inches.

The box is white inside.

It is holow inside.

On their group description, Kristen, Marc, Tracie, and Sean share the writing.

Chapter 12
Explorations with Four Toothpicks

This sequence of activities develops children's spatial reasoning abilities and helps them learn about rotational and mirror symmetry. In these experiences, children are involved with a geometry exploration that has them investigate patterns, sort and classify, solve problems, and play a strategic game.

The activities were introduced in four class periods, beginning with a lesson in which the children searched for all the ways possible to arrange four toothpicks so they are placed either end to end or at right angles. The children were intensely involved with the explorations. Not only did their facility with visualizing spatially increase, but also their involvement with the activities continued long past the class lessons devoted to them.

PATTERNS WITH FOUR TOOTHPICKS

I assembled the materials needed for the first activity—a supply of flat toothpicks, white glue, shallow paper cups for the glue, and construction paper cut into 6-inch-by-9-inch pieces. I used a different color of construction paper for each group, and cut twenty-four pieces of each color.

I gathered the children on the rug to introduce the first activity. "You are to find all the different ways to arrange four toothpicks following two rules," I told the children. "Each toothpick must touch the end of at least one other toothpick, and they must be placed either end to end or so that they make square corners."

I poured some glue into one of the paper cups and asked, "Who can describe a way to arrange the toothpicks that fits the rules?"

Several children raised their hands. I called on Ann. "You can make a square," she said. I did so with four toothpicks and showed the children how to dip the ends of the toothpicks into the glue and place them on a piece of the construction paper.

"You can make an *F*," Michael suggested next. I glued four toothpicks to a piece of construction paper as he directed.

The children offered other suggestions. I did not do any more gluing because I felt they understood how to do it. I wasn't sure, however, that they understood what I meant by "different" shapes. To explain, I drew an *F* on a piece of paper and showed it upside down to the children.

"This shape is the same as the one Michael suggested," I said. "Who can explain why?"

The group tackles the challenge of finding the different arrangements of four toothpicks.

Several children had explanations. "It's upside down." "It's turned around." "It's still an *F*."

Then I drew a shape on another piece of paper, this one a mirror image of an *F*. "This one is also the same as the *F*," I said. "Why do you think that is so?"

While some of the children noticed that it was a backwards *F*, others were perplexed. To help them understand, I turned the paper with the *F* over and held it up to the window. The children could then see it was the same as the mirror image. "If you flip a shape and then it matches another," I explained, "they are considered the same. You can check a shape by drawing it and holding it up to the window."

The children then got to work. This was one of those activities that seemed just right for the children. The problem intrigued them. They were challenged without being frustrated. They took care when gluing and were pleased with the toothpick patterns they were creating. As they worked, they discussed the similarities and differences among the shapes they made.

After about half an hour, Grace, Teddy, Laura, and Jill called me over. "We think we've found them all," Jill reported for the group. "We keep trying and trying, and we keep getting the same shapes." It was nearly the end of math time, and the other groups were still working.

"If you make a record of what you've found, I'll check it against the ones I've found," I told them. They did so, and I took their paper home. I hadn't solved the problem yet myself, but after working on it that evening, I decided that they had indeed found all the possible shapes.

MAKING A DECK OF CARDS

That night, I prepared a sheet on which the children could transfer their toothpick patterns. Though Grace had made a clear and accurate drawing of each of their shapes, I didn't think all the children would be able to do so.

To make the recording sheet, I ruled a piece of paper into sixteen rectangles, each 2 inches by 2-1/2 inches. In each rectangle, I made a 3-by-4 array of dots. This array would accommodate every possible pattern of four toothpicks. I dittoed enough sheets so that each group had one and there were some extras, and I also brought four 5-inch-by-8-inch index cards to class for each group.

Before the children got back to work the next day, I called them back to the rug to show them how to make a deck of cards from their patterns. I showed them the recording sheet Grace had made, and the dot-paper sheet I had designed. "You are to draw each pattern you find in one of these rectangles," I said. I did a few to demonstrate.

"Then cut an index card into four parts," I said, demonstrating that as well. "Cut your dot paper apart and glue each pattern to one of the quarters of the index card. When you've done that, you'll have a deck of cards of all your patterns. Decorate the back of each card—do them all the same—so you can identify them as your group's deck. Then put a rubber band around your deck and set it in the basket."

Again, this was a successful and enjoyable activity for the children. Near the end of the class period, I had Patrick, Ann, Vanessa, and Amber, who had finished their deck first, post the toothpick patterns they had glued on construction paper. They had found the same sixteen as the other group and I had. (This helped convince me that these were indeed the only shapes.)

When the patterns were posted, other groups had a reference against which to check their work. It was fascinating to watch groups check their patterns to see which matched those posted and which were mirror images or rotations. The interaction among the children was exciting to observe.

I took all the children's decks home that night to check them. There were errors in several of them. Even though Patrick, Ann, Vanessa, and Amber had posted sixteen different patterns, they had duplicated one in their recording and had omitted another. In three other groups, there were errors of duplications and omissions.

I attached a note to each deck that had errors. For one, I wrote: "You have an extra card; two shapes are the same." For another: "You're missing the staircase shape, and two others are the same." For two groups, I wrote: "You have doubles of two shapes, and you're missing two."

I explained the notes to the children. Before returning the cards for corrections, however, I gave another task for all the groups. I numbered the patterns posted and asked that the groups number their cards in the same way. The sequence of the numbers had no significance other than identifying the patterns.

"That way," I explained, "when we identify card number 7, for example, we'll all be talking about the same pattern." Not only was this a convenience for the next activity, it also posed another problem for the children. Matching their patterns to those posted required that they exercise their spatial abilities.

There are sixteen different ways to arrange four toothpicks placed either end to end or at right angles. (The numbers are assigned arbitrarily to identify the shapes.)

THE PUT-IN-ORDER PROBLEM

After all groups had completed their decks of cards, I posed the Put-in-Order problem. I asked the groups to arrange their cards in a line so that each pattern could be changed to the next one by moving just one toothpick.

"For example, look at the *T*," I said, referring to the patterns posted. "What other pattern could I make by moving just one toothpick of the *T*."

Several children had suggestions. "You can make the cross." "You can make number 7, the chair." "You can make the *C*." "You can make number 10."

Marina, Kendra and Bryce describe how they solved the problem of arranging the cards so each can be changed to the next one by moving just one toothpick.

Put-in-Order

Marina
Kendra
Bryce

We put the cards in order changing one tooth pick every time. At the end we got stuck we had 11 and we had to change it to 9 so we put 11 in with 13. and 2. It worked this is the order we put them in. 1-16-7-3-15-14-4-13-9-2-12-5-10-8-6-11.

Some had suggestions for how others could be changed. "You can change number 6 to number 8," Michael said.

"Number 12 can be changed to number 13," Erika said.

I then restated the problem for them, and added an additional direction. "You are to make a group record of the order in which you put the cards," I said, "and explain how you solved the problem."

I also made a chart on a large sheet of paper. "There's one additional job," I added. "When you're finished, also record the order of your cards on the chart. We'll look for patterns in your solutions after all groups have solved the problem."

Some groups were confused by the problem and had difficulty getting started. I helped Tara, Andreas, Erika, and Tiare. I gathered their cards, which were scattered on their table, and had Andreas choose one at random and place it face up. "Each of you make that pattern with toothpicks," I directed, "and put the rest of the toothpicks back in the bowl." The four of them did so.

"You'll take turns," I then said, and explained what they were to do. "Tara, you start. Move just one of the toothpicks to make a new pattern. Andreas, Erika, and Tiare, follow with your own toothpicks what Tara does."

Tara moved one toothpick, and the others did the same. "Now, Tara," I said, "find the card with your new pattern on it and place that next to the one Andreas picked." Tara did that, and their sequence was started.

"Now it's Tiare's turn," I said. "Tiare, move a toothpick from the pattern that Tara made to make a new pattern. Everyone else should make the same move." They did so.

"Now, Tiare," I continued, "find the matching card and place it in line."

I continued for Erika's turn. Then, satisfied that they had a way to work and were focused, I left them to continue.

Tara, Andreas, Erika, and Tiare need help getting started on the Put-in-Order problem.

Most of the groups had difficulty getting started. Their frustration resulted in less concentration and more silliness in the classroom than had been exhibited at any time during the past two days. I worked with three other groups as I had with Tara, Andreas, Erika, and Tiare.

Perhaps it would have been better to give the entire class more direction for how to approach the problem before they began work. But I prefer to avoid prescribing one particular approach to a problem. I'd rather the children find their own way. In this case, however, the prescription seemed helpful, even necessary, for some groups. The decision of how much direction to provide differs from situation to situation, and it's always a judgment call for teachers.

All groups ran into difficulty with extra cards at the end. However, my suggestion that they find a place to fit the cards within the line enabled all groups to solve the problem in the class period.

The children were fascinated by the results reported on the chart. There was little similarity among the solutions.

"Let's look at what each group put after card number 1," I said. Five different numbers followed it.

"What other number patterns are possible to make from card number 1 by moving just one toothpick?" I asked, referring to the set of patterns still posted.

The children's concentration and visual ability were remarkable to me. Children were eager to suggest patterns they thought would work. For each one found, I would ask them how they changed it. Some were able to describe which toothpick they would move and how they would move it; others needed to come up and show what they would do. I listed the numbers of the patterns as the children reported them.

Chris discovered another relationship. "Look," he said excitedly, "numbers 1, 3, and 5 all work together."

"What do you mean by that?" I asked.

"See," Chris explained, "you can move one toothpick and change 1 to 3, and 1 to 5, and 3 to 5, and they all work backwards too." This started the children looking for other combinations of three patterns that worked together.

Patrick discovered a triple that wouldn't work. "I found a funny one," he said. "Number 1 can be changed to 4 or 8, but 4 and 8 can't be changed to each other." The class checked that this was so. Patrick's discovery sparked interest in searching for other combinations of patterns with the characteristic he had found. The discussion continued for about twenty minutes. It was one of those rare times when every child had something to contribute to a class discussion.

Groups then reported what they had recorded about the problem. Ann, Vanessa, Patrick, and Amber wrote about their problems and reactions. Vanessa read: *"We had a problem putting the T and the straight line in line so it would work until Ms. Burns came. It was tricky, but interesting."*

Grace, Teddy, and Laura wrote: *"The two ones that were the hardest were 5 and 15. 5 and 15 were hard because they were the last two. They were hard to find a place for and when we did find a place for 5 and 15 we had to move several."*

Tim, Michael, Alana, and Michelle encountered a problem with their deck of cards that I had missed when I had checked them. They reported the problem and how they solved it. They wrote: *"Our group had a problem. We found out that we had two F's. We found that out because Alana made the T, but when we looked for the card, we couldn't find the T, but we found two F's. Then we looked at the board and we looked for the T and when we found it, we looked for the number and it was number 10. Then we looked for our number 10, and it was a F, so we erased it and changed it to a T."*

PLAYING A GAME

The next day, I taught the children a game to play with their patterns. Each group needed its deck of cards and just four toothpicks.

"For a group of four," I told the children, "first, choose any card and make that pattern with the toothpicks. Then shuffle that card back into the pack, and deal all the cards so each player has four." I modeled this with Gabe, Nick, Shaney, and Mairead.

"For groups with three children," I explained, "don't shuffle the beginning pattern card back into the deck. Instead, leave it face up on the table. Then deal the remaining cards." I modeled this with Marina, Kendra, and Bryce.

"How many cards will each child have?" I asked. This wasn't obvious. The children counted and reported they each had five.

"To play," I continued, "place your cards face up in front of you so all cards are visible. The goal is to be the first to play all your cards. Take turns. On your turn, you may discard one card, as long as the pattern on that card can be made by changing the position of just one toothpick on the pattern on the table." I stopped and did a sample to demonstrate this. Then I continued with a few more instructions.

Toothpick Game   Grace Taubenstein
Jan. 14, 1988

In the toothpick game, if I have good cards like ᒧ, ┼, Ḻ, F, ◻, T̩, ┊, or ┠, I try to save them till last. If I didn't save cards that change into a lot of other cards, I'd get stuck. I have an unlikely chance of winning if I get ᒲ.

From playing the Toothpick Game, the children develop a variety of strategies.

"Help one another with moves and discuss the patterns," I said. "If you can't play, you say 'I pass.' Whoever goes out first scores a point. Then start another game. Most of the time, someone wins. Sometimes there is a stalemate, and you have to agree as a group when that happens."

Not only was the game interesting for the children to play, it encouraged them to continue examining the geometric configurations and their flips and rotations. The children continued to play at free time for the rest of the week. Some made decks of cards to take home so they could play with their families. It was a successful experience for all of the children.

Nick Kostopul,
Jan. 14, 1988

Toothpick Game
You don't want the + card because you can only change it to ⊢. You want to have cards that can change to lots of things. For example F ⊢ ⊤ Γ ⌐.

My stratigy is to always put the hardest ones to change down. I learned to keep trying and to do the hardest cards to change.

Ann Macdonald
Jan. 14, 1988

Toothpick Game
My strategy was to win the game!!

There were three cards I did not want to get, number four wich is this one +, number eleven wich is this one | and number twelve with is this one ⌐. I did not want them because they are very hard to change into other paterns.

The cards that you want are number nine wich is this one, □ and number therteen wich is this one, H and number two wich is this one, ↳. These cards made it easy for you __to win.

IV

Probability Activities

Though probability is an important area of study in mathematics, it is not seen as essential to primary math programs and is often overlooked for children in the early grades. There are several reasons for this. Probability is an area of mathematics with which many teachers have had little experience, and we are not generally motivated to teach what we don't fully understand. Also, textbooks do not offer much support for children's exploring probability concepts.

This situation is unfortunate. The lack of attention to probability is a missed opportunity. Probability activities involve children with mathematics explorations that promote their thinking and reasoning skills. From their experiences with probability, children learn to collect, organize, and draw generalizations from data. Also, probability activities help support the development of children's number sense.

Presenting probability concepts to young children is best done by having children involved in experiments of various kinds. From experiments, children have the opportunity to learn that analyzing data can be helpful for making predictions, that some outcomes are more likely than others, and that sample size has an effect on making correct inferences.

Chapter 13 presents an investigation done with first graders in which they collect evidence and then use it to make predictions while having experience with addends of ten. First and second graders experiment with spinners in Chapter 14, and are involved in making predictions based on geometric information. In Chapter 15, third graders make predictions from a random sampling about a population of tiles. Chapter 16 presents a game in which the strategy for playing depends on the rolls of a die; the game also reinforces children's understanding of place-value notation. Chapter 17 contains a collection of probability activities that engaged a class of third graders, showing how a menu is used in a classroom setting.

Chapter 13
The Peek-Box Lesson

The first graders in this lesson were asked to make predictions about the contents of a box based on information they gathered. In this way, the children were given the challenge of drawing inferences from data, a valuable thinking skill that, in this context, was related to a probability experiment. The lesson also provided the children with experience in counting, the concepts of more and less, and the combinations of ten.

INTRODUCING THE LESSON

To prepare for the lesson, I filled six small boxes with marbles, putting seven red and three yellow in each. I cut a hole in one corner of each box, large enough for a marble to slip into and be seen when the box is tilted, but not so large that the marble could fall out. Also, I taped the boxes to discourage the children from looking inside.

"Each of these boxes has ten marbles in it," I told the class. "Some are red, and some are yellow. I filled each box exactly the same way, so no matter which box you take, it has the same number of red marbles and the same number of yellow marbles as all the other boxes. Can anyone guess what I might have put in each box?"

The children were hesitant for a bit. Finally Cynthia volunteered to respond. "You could have 5 red and 5 yellow," she said.

"Let's see if that's possible," I said. I held up first one hand and then the other. "If I had five red and five yellow, I agree that would be ten marbles altogether. So it is possible. Do you know for sure that is what I put in the boxes?" Cynthia and several of the other children either said no or shook their heads.

"How else could I possibly have filled the boxes?" I asked.

Philip raised his hand. "You could have nine red and one yellow," he said.

"How do you know that nine red and one yellow is possible?" I asked. Some of the children started to count on their fingers. Others raised their hands instantly. Philip explained his answer.

"Because nine and one make ten," Philip explained.

"Can you be sure," I asked him, "that is how I really filled the boxes?"

"No, it could be nine yellow and one red," Philip responded.

"Is there any other way I could have filled the boxes?" I asked again. This time, I called on Richmond.

"Did you put in ten red and ten yellow?" he asked.

A demonstration helps the children see how to shake and tilt the box so a marble falls into the corner hole.

A few of the others said that couldn't be, that there weren't that many marbles in the boxes. Richmond didn't seem to understand why his guess couldn't be possible.

"How many fingers do you have?" I asked Richmond. He knew he had ten fingers.

"And how many toes do you have?" I continued. He knew he had ten toes.

I then explained, "If I put ten red marbles and ten yellow marbles into each box, that would be the same as putting in one marble for each of your fingers and one marble for each of your toes. That's too many. I put in only ten marbles, one for each of your fingers. So I know there can't be ten red and ten yellow."

Though other children nodded in agreement with this explanation, Richmond didn't seem to understand. That did not disturb me. It was only the second month in the school year, and I knew many of the children had not as yet learned their combinations of ten. A class discussion such as this, however, can stimulate children to think about the combinations of ten while helping me assess which children do and which do not have such understanding.

Using fingers to verify thinking may trouble some teachers. Fingers have been thought of as a crutch for children, a crutch they should not be encouraged to use. Rather than thinking of fingers as a crutch, however, it is more constructive to see them as one of many possible tools for aiding thinking, justifying an answer, and making sense out of numbers. What better way to learn to visualize the combinations of ten than to use some concrete referent, and what more convenient referent is there than fingers?

I continued questioning what could be in the boxes for just a few minutes more, not wanting to belabor something that was too abstract for some of the children. I then explained to the children what they were to do.

"How could we find out what I really put in the boxes?" I asked. This seemed obvious to the children, and they answered almost in a chorus, "Open them."

"Yes, that would work," I said, "and we'll do that at the end of the week. But before we do that, I want you to try a mathematical experiment to help you guess."

I then demonstrated for the children how to tilt a box to let a marble fall into the corner hole. "What color is the marble?" I asked. The children could see that the marble in the open corner was red. I shook the box and again tilted it so a marble fell into the corner hole. It was red this time also. I repeated the process several more times, getting a representation of red and yellow marbles.

I showed the children the recording sheets I had prepared, half-sheets of ditto paper with ten circles on each. The children were to color the circles with red and yellow crayons to show which color of marble they saw when they tilted the box. Also, they were to write how many reds and yellows had come up after ten peeks.

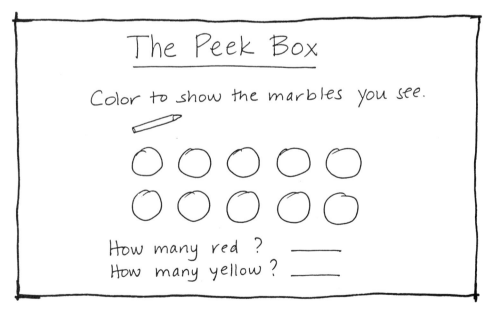

The children use the recording sheet to show how many red and yellow marbles come up in ten peeks.

"You will shake, tilt, and peek ten times," I explained to the children, "and record what you see on a recording sheet. Each time you tilt the box, color a circle either red or yellow."

I modeled this for them. After three tilts, I had colored two circles red and one yellow. I then asked, "How many more tilts do I need to do in order to complete my sheet?" Some of the children knew; most guessed. I had them count the uncolored circles with me.

"I colored three, and I have to color seven more to complete all ten," I summarized, another chance to focus the children on combinations of ten. I continued the experiment until all the circles were colored. I wound up with six red circles and four yellow circles.

"When you've colored in all your circles," I explained, "count how many red circles and how many yellow circles you colored. Write those numbers on your recording sheet in the spaces provided." I did this on my recording sheet.

"When you're finished, put your recording sheet in the Peek-Box envelope," I said. I had labeled a 9-inch-by-12-inch envelope and tacked it onto the bulletin board.

With a last reminder that they were not to open the boxes yet, that we would do that together on Friday, I put out the materials. This task was one of several the children could choose from during math time. Because there were only six boxes, I reviewed the need to wait if there were already six children using them. The children were comfortable with this concept from their experience with limits as to how many children could be at a learning station at one time.

SUMMARIZING THE ACTIVITY

By Friday, each student had completed the experiment. I gathered the children together to take a look at the results. For this discussion, I ruled three columns on the chalkboard and labeled them—more red than yellow, same red as yellow, more yellow than red.

I distributed the recording sheets to the children. Because the children hadn't put their names on their sheets, it did not matter whose sheet they were given. I asked the children to look at the recording sheet they had.

"Does anyone have a recording sheet with the same number of red colored in as yellow?" I asked. Three children raised their hands. "Bring them up," I said, "and we'll tape them to the class chart in the column for the same number of red as yellow."

When they were posted, I had the children count with me to see how many red and yellow circles were colored on each recording sheet. It didn't seem obvious to all the children that each would have to be the same, with five red and five yellow colored in.

Next I asked, "Does anyone have a recording sheet with more yellow circles than red circles colored in?" Again, three children raised their hands. I asked each to report how many were colored on the sheets they had.

The children post the recording sheets on a class chart.

Nancy reported first, "I have six yellow and four red." She came up and taped hers in the column for more yellow than red. Michael and Melissa had the same results to report. They taped their sheets to the chart.

"Who has a recording sheet with more red circles than yellow circles colored in?" I then asked. The remaining children in the class raised their hands. I had the children come up, a small group at a time, and tape their recording sheets in the column for more red than yellow. I organized this so that ten children taped their recording sheets one underneath the other. I then had the other seven tape their recording sheets in a column next to the first ten.

Together, the class and I counted the recording sheets that had more red circles than yellow colored in. "There are seventeen recording sheets here," I said. "Ten here and seven more make seventeen." This was an opportunity to relate seventeen to tens and ones.

"What do you notice about how many red and yellow circles are colored on these sheets?" I asked the children.

"They're all different," Tina said.

"What do you mean by that?" I asked.

"See that one has one yellow circle," she explained, coming up to point at one of the recording sheets, "and that one has two."

Other children chimed in. "I see one with three yellows," Michael said.

"There's another one with one yellow," Cynthia said.

Some of the children began to come to the board to point out recording sheets. I called the class back to attention. I asked Carmen to sit down and told all the others to stay seated as well. I appreciated their interest and enthusiasm, but I wanted to settle them again and focus on the information in an orderly way.

When they were seated, we looked at the recording sheets and found all the different numbers of red and yellow circles that were colored in. There were papers with nine red and one yellow, eight red and two yellow, seven and three, and six and four. Not only were the children getting information which could lead them to make a prediction about what might really be in the boxes, they were having more experience with some of the combinations of ten.

"Looking at all the papers posted on the chart," I asked, "do you think there are more red marbles or more yellow marbles in the boxes?" Most of the children responded that there were more red. When asked to explain why, I got two kinds of answers: "Because there are more on the chart" and "Because that was what I got." For some of the children, their individual results were more important to them even though I had asked that they examine the chart to decide.

"I think that it is possible that there are more yellow marbles than red marbles in the boxes," I said. "Who can explain why I think that?"

Melissa volunteered to answer. "Because that was what I got when I did it," she said.

"I had more yellow circles on the sheet I put up," Darrell said.

There were no other responses.

I then asked, "Could there be the same number of red as yellow marbles in the boxes?"

"It could be, but I don't think so," Richard said.

"Why don't you think so?" I asked.

"Because of the chart," Richard replied.

Richard was comfortable using the evidence on the chart to decide. However, this was not true for all of his classmates. Many children still tied their reasoning to what their own particular results had been. This is not surprising for first graders. As children mature, they are more likely to use evidence from a source such as the class chart rather than to rely on their own experience. Taking note of who did and did not make inferences from the class evidence gave me additional insights into individual children's thinking.

I then told them they were each to predict what they thought was really inside the boxes. "I'm going to give you each a new recording sheet," I said, holding up a sample. "It says, 'What's inside the Peek Box?' In the space on top, you are to show what you think really is in the box. In the space underneath, you are to show what other combinations you think could be in the box." I reviewed the directions with the children and then gave them the sheets to fill out.

After all the children had completed recording their predictions, I gathered them together to open a box. They counted the marbles and found there were 7 red and 3 yellow. The children cheered, not because they had predicted correctly (only two children had), but for the event itself.

"Can we do it again?" Randy asked.

"Yes, that's possible," I responded. The children cheered again.

"But you'll have to give me a while to make new boxes," I added. Doing the activity again later in the year would be a way to assess children's growth.

THE CHILDREN'S PREDICTIONS

I did not discuss with the class the final predictions the children had made. I did not give validation to those children who had predicted correctly. This was not necessary because opening the box provided the actual feedback. Nor did I point out errors to those children who had made incorrect or unreasonable predictions.

I avoided doing that because the purpose of the lesson was not for children to master a particular skill. Instead, it was a learning opportunity designed to contribute to the children's development of mathematics understanding and to keep them motivated and interested in mathematics.

Calling attention to and praising some children for correct responses runs the risk of giving the children the message that the right answer is what is most important. It can also contribute to making those who answered incorrectly feel that they are unsuccessful learners. While this feedback may be appropriate when children are practicing a skill, it would not be appropriate in this lesson.

It is more constructive and supportive in an activity such as this for the teacher to examine the children's papers for the purpose of learning something about each child's mathematical development and understanding. The written work revealed which children were capable of offering reasonable predictions, which children were and which were not making use of the data collected in the children's samples, and which children were not ready to deal with a number as large as ten. Their written work was very useful for me, too, in planning additional learning experiences to help the children.

In this instance, there was a large range in the children's recordings. When showing what they thought was in the box, nine of the twenty-three children drew possibilities for which there were more red marbles than yellow marbles. Four children drew five red and five yellow. Three other children were one off in their drawings, showing seven red and four yellow, eight red and one yellow, and three red and six yellow. The other seven children drew ten red and either one or two yellow, showing that they thought there would be more red, but not able to incorporate the information that there were ten marbles in all.

In the space allowed for the children to draw what also could be in the boxes, there were all sorts of answers, some drawing one possibility and others drawing two or three possible combinations. As I expected, no child seemed interested in finding all the possibilities, a task far beyond the developmental level of most six-year-olds.

During this experience, all of the children were actively involved and thinking—important goals for all math lessons.

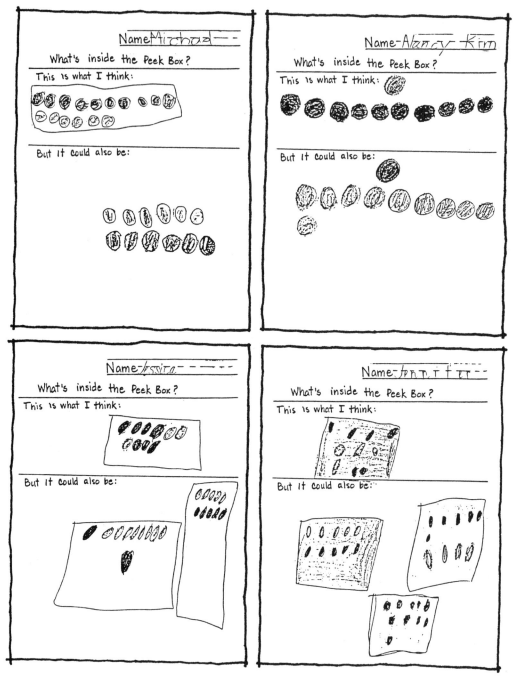

The children's predictions provide useful information for assessing their under-standing and planning additional learning experiences.

Chapter 14
Experiments with Spinners

Two different ways to involve children with spinner experiments are presented in this chapter. Each is a variation on helping children learn that some outcomes in an experiment can be more likely than others. First graders are involved with this idea by comparing what happens with two different spinners; second graders concentrate on the results from one spinner.

In addition to involving children with probability concepts, these spinner activities provide experience with collecting information and representing it graphically, writing numerals, and comparing quantities. Each of the activities is suitable for children in grades 1, 2, and 3.

The lesson with first graders spanned several days. First, the children were taught how to conduct an experiment with each of two spinners. In a follow-up summary time, the children examined the class results and discussed several ideas relating to concepts of probability.

The second graders made their own spinners, an aspect of the lesson that provided them with a valuable experience in following directions. They then used their spinners for an experiment and posted their results. The results were analyzed in a class discussion.

Directions for making the spinners are included in the section describing the second-grade lesson.

A LESSON WITH FIRST GRADERS

I prepared for this lesson by making two different spinners for the children to use. Each spinner had the numbers 1, 2, 3, and 4 on it. I made one spinner in orange, equally dividing the face into fourths and writing one number in each segment. The other had a yellow face, half of which was devoted to the number 3, with the other half divided into three equal segments, numbered 1, 2, and 4. I made eight spinners of each type.

I also prepared recording sheets for the children. Each sheet was to be used for two experiments. I duplicated enough sheets so that there was one for each child, plus extras for children who might want to do more.

I posed a question to the class. "Where have you used spinners before?" I asked. Several children responded that they had used them in games. Philip added, "You use them to pick a winning number."

I showed the children the spinners they would be using and explained to them what they were going to do. "Each of you will do two experiments," I

Two different spinners are used for the activity.

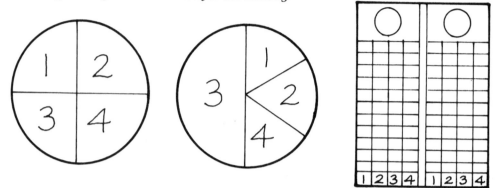

said, "one with the orange spinner and one with the yellow spinner. I'll show you how."

I showed the children a recording sheet. "You start by drawing a picture of the face of the spinner in the circle at the top and coloring it yellow or orange," I explained, and demonstrated this for the children. I thought that drawing the faces would help focus the children on the differences between the spinners.

"Then you spin the spinner and see which number comes up," I continued. "Write the number that comes up in the correct column. This time a 3 came up, so I'll write it in the column above the 3 that is already there." I wrote it for the children to see.

"Then you spin again," I said, "and write that number where it belongs." I continued doing that, emphasizing for the children that when a number came up for the first time, they were to write it at the bottom of a new column.

"Keep doing this until one number gets to the finish line," I explained. For my experiment, the number 2 reached the top of its column first. The children watched with fascination as the numbers teeter-tottered up the columns. Some rooted for the particular numbers to "win."

I then posed several questions to focus the children on the spinners. "What's different about these two spinners?" I asked, holding up a yellow and an orange spinner.

The children commented on several things. "There's more space for the 3 on the yellow one." "The spaces for the 1, 2, and 4 on the yellow one are all small." "The orange one is divided up evenly."

"What's alike about the two spinners?" I asked.

Again, the children noticed several things. "They have the same numbers on them." "They're both round." "They're circles."

"Which number do you think will reach the finish line first when you spin the yellow one?" I asked. Several children immediately volunteered that the 3 would finish first, and most nodded their agreement. "Its space is bigger," Hassan explained.

"What about when you spin the orange spinner?" I continued. Again, the children made predictions. This time, however, their predictions varied. When children offered predictions, I asked them to explain why they thought it was so. Their answers varied. "Three, because it is my favorite number." "Four, because it's biggest." "Two, because it won when you did it." "Three," with a shrug for an explanation.

I then reviewed what they were to do, including a few additional directions. "When you do your experiments," I said, "you will work with a partner. You'll each have a recording sheet for your two experiments and will start with one spinner. Work together. First one of you spins and the other writes the numbers that come up. Then you switch jobs and do another experiment, so the other can record on his or her sheet."

By organizing the children into pairs, each has the help of a classmate. This provides support for those who might have difficulty working alone. Also, in this way, I needed fewer spinners, which made my preparation easier. I had enough spinners so each pair could have one, and there were three extras left for children who finished more quickly.

I showed the children the two boxes I had set out. "This box is for the spinners," I explained. "I'll start by giving a spinner to you and your partner. Return it to this box when you're done with it and take the other kind."

I then explained about the recording sheets. "When you've each finished your two experiments, your completed recording sheets go in this box," I said. "Before putting it in the box, however, cut it apart so that each experiment is on a separate sheet."

I also talked with the class about the need to report what really comes up. From past experience, I knew that for some children, fulfilling their own prediction can take precedence over recording accurate results. "These are to be scientific experiments," I told them. "The purpose is for us to learn something about these spinners and to see what that can help us learn about mathematics. It's very important that you do the experiment carefully, being sure to record the number that really comes up each time."

I added one more direction. "Also, as soon as one number reaches the top of its column, you should stop that experiment. If you want to do more, you can get another recording sheet and do another experiment." I also knew from past experience that some first graders get so involved with spinning and writing the numbers in the boxes that they will continue until their entire recording sheet is filled.

I then passed out a spinner and two recording sheets to each pair of children. The children got to work.

SUMMARIZING THE EXPERIENCE

I provided time during this day and the following one for all the children to complete their experiments. When they had all done so, I had Jessica and Carmen sort the papers into two piles, separating the records of the two different spinners.

I called the class together for a discussion. I began by explaining to the children how Jessica and Carmen had sorted the papers. I picked up the pile of papers for the yellow spinner, the one with half the face numbered 3. "I'm going to look at each graph record in this pile," I explained to the class, "and

Carmen and Michael do the spinner experiments together.

read off the number that finished first each time. You listen carefully as I do this. When I've gone through the pile, I'm going to ask if you can tell me if one number came up more often than the others and which number it was."

I read the numbers. On all but three of the papers, 3 finished first. As I was reading the results, the children cheered each time I read a 3. They were enthusiastically in support of 3 finishing first.

When I had gone through the entire pile, I asked the children what they now knew. They knew for sure that 3 had "won" most often, and several explained why this made sense. Danny's explanation was typical. "The 3 takes up more space," he said.

I then repeated the procedure for the pile of recording sheets for the orange spinner, with equal regions for 1, 2, 3, and 4. When I completed reading the numbers which had reached the finish line on each sheet, the children could not tell which number I had called most often.

"How could we find out?" I asked.

Some children shrugged, while others had suggestions.

"We have to see them," Felipe said.

"We have to count up," Miriam added.

I taped the recording sheets across the chalkboard in four rows, one for each of the numbers 1, 2, 3, and 4. By lining up the sheets in that way, I constructed a graph that made it easy to see that the number 2 came up most often. The number 3, however, came up only two fewer times.

I then asked the children questions to direct them to think about what this large graph showed. After each question, I allowed some time for thinking before calling on children to share their thoughts. Questions included: "Which number came up most often?" "Which number came up least often?" "How many record sheets are posted altogether?" "How many more times did 4 come up than 3?"

"Why do you think 2 finished most often?" I also asked. The two prevailing explanations seemed to be "Because it's biggest" and "I don't know."

To probe further, I asked, "If you each did the experiment again, and we posted your recording sheets, which number do you think might finish first the second time?" Some children predicted 2, because it had won the first time. Others predicted 3, because it had won on the other spinner. Some had no idea. Others still clung to predictions of their favorite number.

I then focused them on some of the individual results. "Look at this one," I said. "Even though 2 finished first, the number 1 is just one behind. It almost finished first. And look at this one. The number 4 finished first, but the numbers 3 and 2 are very close behind. What do you notice on others?" The children looked over the record sheets posted, raising their hands to report what they noticed.

To compare these observations with those from the other spinner, I passed out a completed recording sheet for the yellow spinner to each child. They looked at the one they were given and compared it to the ones their neighbors had. Children noticed that on most of these sheets, the numbers 1, 2, or 4 were not major contenders for finishing first and that 3 was generally a clear winner.

Although the children were able to explain why 3 came up most often, it was difficult for them to explain how these sheets compared with the ones posted. They had difficulty verbalizing the differences. This is not surprising for first graders. They need a great deal of experience in thinking, reasoning, and expressing their ideas.

The lesson gave the children a beginning experience with probability, with the opportunity to learn that in some situations, some outcomes are more likely than others. The lesson gave me the opportunity to learn more about how individual children reason using evidence and what they understand.

AN EXTENSION INVESTIGATION

Suppose you were playing a board game that involved racing around a track for a finish line. You had a marker, which you moved the number of spaces that came up when spinning a spinner. You have two choices for spinners—either the yellow spinner or the orange spinner. Which spinner would you choose? Or doesn't it make any difference? Children might enjoy creating such board games and trying this experiment.

Another extension—this one for teachers: Which spinner would you choose for the board game if the yellow spinner had a 4 on one half instead of a 3? Or a 1, or a 2? Using spinners has many opportunities for further study.

The second graders began their spinner investigation by making their own spinners. I collected all the materials I needed and modeled for the children exactly what they were to do. Also, I duplicated directions for making a spinner so that each group of four children could refer to it as they worked. I also made a few examples for them to examine.

For each group of four children, I assembled four paper clips, two 5-inch-by-8-inch index cards, and a 9-inch-by-12-inch sheet of tag on which I had duplicated four circular spinner faces. On each circle, half was numbered 3, and the other half was divided equally and numbered 1 and 2. I also had two sheets of paper ruled into one-inch squares for each group as well as scissors and masking tape.

I began by showing the class one of the spinners I had already made. I gave it a healthy spin and received a chorus of "Oooohs." The children were impressed with how fast and long the spinner spun. "It's spinning so fast you can't even see the numbers," Melissa said.

"I'm going to teach you how to make a spinner like this," I told the children, "and then show you how to use it for an experiment. After I do that, you'll each get to make a spinner and do the experiment."

The children were keenly interested and watched carefully. I knew that making the spinner would be easier for some than for others. By having them work in groups, the children would be able to help one another when they needed help.

Before modeling how they were to do the experiment with their spinners, I asked the children which number they thought would come up when I spun the spinner. Many hands were raised. I called on Becky.

"I think 3 will come up," she said.

"Why do you think that?" I asked.

"Because it takes up more space than the other numbers. I takes up half," she explained.

I directed another question to the class. "Is it possible that when I spin the spinner a 1 or a 2 will come up?" I asked.

There were many nods. Jason raised his hand. "It could happen because it won't always land on 3," he said.

I then described the experiment to the children. "You each are going to try an experiment in which you'll use your spinner to find out which numbers come up when you spin it many times. I'll do the experiment first to show you what you are to do."

I showed the children how they were to make a recording sheet. Instead of duplicating them, as I had done for the first graders, I showed them how to cut their recording sheets from the squared paper. I cut a strip that was three columns wide and the length of the paper. It had ten rows on it.

"Why do you think I cut a strip with three columns?" I asked.

Many hands were raised. I called on Sara. "Because there are three numbers on the spinner," she explained.

HOW TO MAKE A SPINNER THAT REALLY SPINS

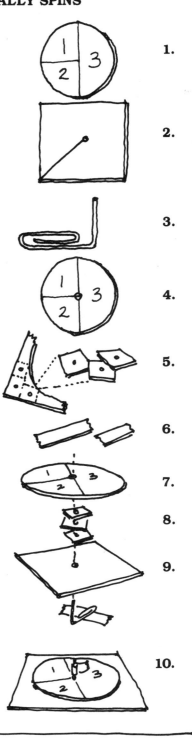

1. Cut a circle from the tag.

2. Cut a 5-inch-by-8-inch index card in half. Draw a line on one half from one corner toward the center.

3. Take a paper clip and bend just the outside up. This part should point straight up when the paper clip is lying flat on the desk.

4. Poke a hole in the center of the circle (be exact) and near the center of the half of the index card.

5. Take a scrap left from cutting out the circle, and poke three holes in it about an inch apart. Then cut three small squares so that each has a hole in the center of it. These will be used as washers.

6. Cut two pieces of masking tape, one a little more than an inch, one a little shorter.

7. Assemble the spinner by first poking the paper clip through the index card from the blank side. Tape the paper clip on the bottom to hold it in place.

8. Then put the three washers on the part of the paper clip pointing up.

9. Put the spinner face on.

10. Add a piece of tape to cover the point of the paper clip. Now it's ready to spin.

"That's exactly right," I responded. "When I spin the spinner, I will record each number that comes up, writing the 1s in the first column, the 2s in the second, and the 3s in the third. You spin until one number reaches the top of its column. Then you'll have a graph that shows how many times each number came up."

I then demonstrated what I had said. When I had completed the experiment, 3 was at the top of its row, 2 was only one square behind, and there were four 1s. I then told the children what they were to do with their graphs. I wrote 1, 2, and 3 on the chalkboard, ruling lines to define a space under each number.

"When you've completed your experiment," I said, "tape your graph under the number that reached the top of its column." I taped mine under the number 3.

"What do you think the board will look like after all of you have posted your results?" I asked.

"They'll all be under the 3," Peter said.

"No, look," Melissa said, referring to my graph record sheet. "Two almost won."

Randy had a comment, "I think mostly 3 will win."

"We'll see after you've all done this," I said. I gave them my speech about this being a scientific experiment and that they were to be careful to report exactly what came up. Then I asked for questions. There were several.

"What do you do if it lands on a line?" Maria asked. It was the kind of question I've come to expect from Maria, who likes to be sure to do things perfectly.

"Just spin it again," I said.

Jason had a question. "Can we do it more than once?"

"I want you to make only one spinner," I responded. "But if there is time, you can do another experiment and post it. The more experiments we have, the more evidence we can examine."

"Do we do the experiments together?" Abby asked.

"You each need to make your own spinner and do your own experiment," I said. "But you are to help anyone in your group who needs assistance."

"What if there's a tie between two numbers?" Jenny asked.

That question surprised me, and it took me a minute to think about how to answer it. Joshua beat me to it, however. "There can't be a tie," he said. "You have to stop when one gets to the top."

Jenny seemed satisfied.

There were no more questions. I had set all the materials out on the counter, and gave the children one more direction. "Choose one person from your group to come and get all the materials you need," I explained. "Line up behind one another, and I'll help you take what you need from the counter." In this way, the materials were distributed in an orderly manner. Also, it focused the groups on working together.

Though some children needed help, everyone did remarkably well. The major difficulties involved poking holes with the paper clip and assembling all the pieces correctly. The children were delighted with their spinners, and by recess time, all but two had posted their results, and some had done the experiment again.

Making their own spinners gives the second graders experience with following directions.

SUMMARIZING THE EXPERIENCE

After the children returned from recess, those who hadn't finished completed their experiments, while the rest of the children cleaned up the scraps and put away the materials. I then gathered the class together to discuss the results.

"As you predicted," I began, "3 got to the top of the column more often. Let's count and see how many record sheets were posted under each number." We counted together. There were four record sheets posted under the number 1, three under the number 2, and twenty-four under the number 3.

Michael raised his hand. "That one's in the wrong place. See, 2 won," he said, pointing to a record sheet under the 3.

He was right, and I moved it to its proper location. Sara spotted another, also posted under the 3, which belonged under the 1. I moved that one as well. That seemed to correct the problems. Now there were five, four, and twenty-two posted under the 1, 2, and 3.

"Who can explain why 3 got to the top most often?" I asked. Though we had talked about this a bit before doing the experiments, I was interested in what they had to say now that they had experience. All the children who wanted to were given the opportunity to explain their thoughts.

I did not comment on their explanations. After each one, I asked if anyone had a different idea or a different way to explain something that had already been reported. My goal was to give as many children as possible the chance to verbalize their thinking. I also encouraged them to listen to one another to see if that gave them any new ideas.

About half the children offered their thoughts. Some children talked about the spinner in general terms. "Three has the most space." "Three is half of the spinner." "The space with 3 is bigger than the space with 1 or 2." "Three is the same as 1 and 2 together."

Other children focused more on their own particular experience. "It could be luck, because I had 2 come up most." "One hardly comes up at all; I only got two 1s." "I got 3 the most times on my spinner."

ANOTHER INVESTIGATION

I pursued the activity a bit further, introducing an additional investigation. I removed a graph record sheet on which five 1s, four 2s, and ten 3s were recorded.

"This graph record sheet shows results that look like what the spinner should do," I said to the class. "Let me explain why. The 3s are at the top, and, as most of you said, it makes sense for the 3 to finish first. Also, the 1s and 2s came up just about as often as each other. Why do I think this is what the spinner should do?"

Melissa had an answer. "Because the 1 and 2 take up the same amount of space on the spinner," she said. Others nodded their agreement.

"The 3 came up ten times on this record," I continued. "The 1 and 2 together came up just about as many times, nine times altogether. What can you say about that?"

Joshua had a comment. "The 1 and the 2 on the spinner take up as much space together as the 3 does," he said. Others agreed.

I then structured a way to compare how often 1, 2, and 3 came up on all the data they had generated. "Watch now as I start another experiment," I said. I took two other graph record sheets down from the chalkboard and cut each of the three I now had into three columns. Then, using masking tape, I taped the 1s, 2s, and 3s into three long strips.

"If we did this with all the graph record sheets, how would the strips of 1s, 2s, and 3s compare?" I asked the class.

The responses went from "I don't know" to "The 3 would be the longest" to "The 1 and 2 would be about the same, but maybe four or five squares different."

I told the children that each group was to make strips from three record sheets, and then we would combine the groups' strips together. Though the cutting and assembling of the long strips excited all the children, not all really understood the purpose. Still, it seemed worthwhile to challenge those who were ready to consider the question and to introduce the possibility to the others.

I passed out three sheets to each group, leaving extras for the groups who finished more quickly. The children did this activity well. Finally, we had them all to compare. With the children's help, I taped their strips across the top of the chalkboard.

The row of 3s extended past the chalkboard to the corner of the room and then continued for about one-third of the adjacent wall. The rows of 1s and 2s were just about the same length as each other; there were nine more 1s than 2s. The results were not exactly in the proportion of the spinner, however. The strips of 1s and 2s were each more than half of the strip of 3s. Still, the results were impressive.

"That's pretty good," Peter said. I thought so too.

Chapter 15
Tile Sampling

L earning to interpret information and to use it to draw conclusions is an important aspect of being able to think critically. Children gain experience with these thinking skills in this lesson through a sampling investigation with Color Tiles.

The lesson was done with a class of third graders. The children had not had a great deal of previous experience collecting and interpreting data. However, it is from activities of this kind that understanding will develop and children will be better able to make generalizations.

HOW MANY TILES OF EACH COLOR?

"I've put tiles in this bag," I said to the class, shaking the brown-paper lunch bag I had used. "In this activity, you're going to guess how many of each color I put in." Several hands immediately went up, children who were ready and eager to guess.

"Before I ask you to guess," I said, "I want to give you some clues that you can use." The hands went down.

"My first clue is that I put twelve tiles into the bag," I said. Hands went up again.

"I'm going to give you another clue," I continued. The hands went down.

"I used only red and yellow tiles," I said. Hands went up again.

In this lesson, I wanted the children to have the experience of using information to make predictions. I didn't want to encourage random guessing. So before calling on any child to guess, I asked, "Who can tell me one thing you know for sure about what is in the bag?" I waited, giving the children time to think.

Finally, I called on Nick. "There are tiles," he said.

Next I called on Michelle. "There are twelve of them," she said.

"Some are red and some are yellow," Bayard added.

I wrote on the board: There are twelve tiles. Some are red and some are yellow. Then I asked, "Who has an idea about what might be in the bag, even though you can't be totally sure?" Now I was willing to entertain their guesses.

"It could be six red and six yellow," Teddy said. I wrote "6 r and 6 y" on the board, checking with the class to make sure they realized that r and y were abbreviations for red and yellow.

"Does six plus six equal twelve?" I asked. The children nodded.

Patrick had another possibility. "Seven red and five yellow," he said, and I wrote that below Teddy's suggestion.

"Do seven and five add to twelve?" I asked. Again, the children nodded.

Vanessa spoke next. "Eight red and four yellow," she said, and I wrote it down.

The children continued giving me possibilities, following the orderly pattern that Teddy, Patrick, and Vanessa had begun. After each child gave a possibility, I asked the class to check that the numbers added to twelve. The list now contained:

6 r and 6 y
7 r and 5 y
8 r and 4 y
9 r and 3 y
10 r and 2 y
11 r and 1 y

Andreas raised his hand next. He said, "Twelve red tiles and no yellow tiles." I added "12 r and 0 y" to the list.

"Is twelve plus zero equal to twelve?" I asked. The class nodded yes.

"But this can't be one of the possibilities," I said.

"Oh, I know," Jill called out. "They'd be all red, and you said there were red and yellow in the bag."

Andreas agreed that twelve red and zero yellow was not a possibility, and I erased it from the list. The class was silent for a moment.

Michael then raised his hand. "You can do them backwards," he said, "like one red and eleven yellows." That started the class off again, and they found the rest. Finally, all eleven possibilities were on the board.

"Now that you know what could be in the bag," I told the class, "we're going to collect some information that can help you guess what really is in the bag."

I wrote red and yellow on the board, with recording space below each. I then explained how we would collect information. I asked Gabe, who was seated near where I was standing, to reach into the bag without looking, withdraw a tile, and show it to the class. He did so, drawing out a red tile. "Now put the tile back into the bag," I said. I made a tally mark in the red column.

"We'll do this twelve times," I continued, "and then we'll talk about what the information shows." I called for a volunteer to do the tallying, and chose Laura.

Before another child reached into the bag, I shook it. "I think it's a good idea to shake the bag between each draw," I said. "Why do you suppose I think that?" Children had different ways to express their thinking. All their ideas centered around the idea that it would mix up the tiles so that they wouldn't be taking out the same one each time.

I went around the room, having children draw tiles. After twelve samples, there were six tallies in each column. I then asked the children what they thought might be in the bag. I also asked them each to explain their predictions.

"I think there are six red and six yellow," Vanessa said, "because that's what the chart says."

Laura tallies on the chalkboard as each child draws a tile from the bag.

Nick had a different thought. "I think there are more yellows, like seven yellows and five reds," he said, "because four yellows were picked in a row, and I think that counts."

"I think there are seven reds and five yellows," Erika said, "because that seems right."

After all the children who wanted to had expressed their opinions, I had the class repeat the sampling again. The next twelve draws produced seven red and five yellow. Twelve additional draws again produced seven red and five yellow. During this procedure, I would stop from time to time to ask the children how many more draws we needed that round to get to twelve. This was just a way to slip in some reinforcement of basic facts.

After completing the three sets of twelve samples, I again had children predict what was in the bag. Their opinions were similar to their opinions after just twelve draws. Some still felt six and six was right. Others felt there were more red. Still others felt there were more yellow.

Many of the children were interested in offering their predictions and explaining their reasoning. It was interesting to note that their reasons were less often based on the information from the sampling than on other thoughts. "I think people were taking the same tiles over and over." "I just think I'm right." "Because you shook the bag."

The children were curious and eager to learn what was in the bag. I spilled the tiles, revealing that there were eight red tiles and four yellow tiles. There were some cheers and some groans.

"Since there were eight red tiles and four yellow tiles," I said, "how can you explain the information we gathered from drawing tiles out of the bag?" Again the children had different thoughts. "It could be luck." "It depends if you take a tile from the top or dig down." "It could be different next time."

I repeated the activity, again with a bag of twelve tiles, but this time the bag contained two red, two yellow, and eight blue. "In this bag," I told the children, "I put twelve tiles, and I used three colors—red, yellow, and blue. We'll try the same experiment and see how you can predict this time."

I did not have them list what could be in the bag because I thought there are just too many possibilities for third graders to handle. Also, I was more interested in focusing them on using information to draw conclusions.

Three sets of twelve draws produced the following results:

red	yellow	blue
1	1	10
1	2	9
3	3	6

"It's hard to tell," Teddy said.

I then had the class add the numbers in each column. We did this as a class, adding mentally. Michael recorded the totals.

	red	yellow	blue
TOTALS	5	6	25

"What do you feel you now know absolutely for sure?" I asked.

Patrick was eager and confident to respond. "There aren't as many reds as blues," he said.

"Who else knows something they're absolutely sure of?" I asked again.

Jill offered, "There are more blue tiles than yellow tiles."

Grace said, "There are six blues and three yellows and three reds."

"I think that reds and yellows are the same, or maybe one off," Teddy said.

"Suppose I were to ask," I continued, "if you were sure enough about what you said that you were willing to bet all your recesses until the end of the year." I directed this at Patrick first. "Would you bet your recesses, Patrick?" I asked.

"Yes," he said, with certainty.

"What about you, Jill?" I asked.

"Yes," she also said.

"Grace?"

"No, I don't think so," she said, shaking her head.

"Teddy?"

"No way," he answered.

I then gave the children a writing assignment to do in their groups. I asked them to discuss what they thought was in the bag and to explain their thoughts in writing.

Grace, Teddy, Jill, and Laura had a split of opinions in their group. While Grace and Jill based their predictions on the data, Teddy and Laura were more convinced by their own experience. Their group wrote: *"Grace and Jill think there are 6 blues, 3 yellows and 3 reds. Laura and Teddy think there are 5 blues, 4 yellows and 3 reds. Teddy and Laura think this because they picked blue up more and yellows a little more than red. Grace and Jill think this because there were a lot of blues picked out."*

Michael, Michelle, Timothy, and Alana did not make a numerical prediction, but focused their comments on the effects of the position of the tiles in the bag. They wrote: *"We think there are more blues than reds or yellows. We think this because all the yellows and reds are down at the botom of the bag and the blues are at the top and when you shake the bag all the blues block the reds and yellows from coming up to the top. Most of the people take the blocks off the top and that's why more people picked up blue than red or yellow."*

From Nick, Mairead, Shaney, and Gabe: *"We think there are 6 blues, 3 reds, 3 yellows. We think this because 3 + 3 = 6. 6 + 6 = 12. And every body almost picked blue so there must be more blue than red and yellow."*

While the groups were working, Amber came to me to complain that Patrick wasn't listening to her idea. I joined her group to deal with the problem. Helping children learn to work cooperatively requires attention to situations such as this one. Children need help focusing on their task and on their communication.

Grace, Teddy, Jill, and Laura's paper explains their different opinions.

Patrick was recording for the group. "Everyone agrees with what I'm writing except for Amber," he said.

"They didn't listen to me," Amber complained.

"You weren't talking with us," Patrick responded. "You were up at the board looking at the numbers."

"I was trying to figure something out," Amber defended herself.

Vanessa and Ann watched this exchange without commenting.

I interrupted Patrick and Amber and said, "Listen to me for just a minute. What I hear from Amber is that she has some thoughts that the group hasn't heard yet. What I hear from Patrick is that Amber wasn't contributing her thoughts. What can you as a group do about this situation?"

Vanessa, less emotionally involved than Patrick or Amber, offered a suggestion. "Amber can tell us what she thinks," she said.

"But nobody wanted to listen," Amber said, still upset.

"You were up at the board," Patrick argued.

"Wait, wait, wait," I said. "Let's talk about now, not about before. Remember that it is the group's responsibility to make sure everyone gets listened to. Also, if you have something to say, it's your responsibility to ask the group to listen. I have a suggestion. Patrick, how about reading what you've written so everyone in the group hears what's on the paper so far? Then you each take a turn to say what you think. Then, Amber, you can explain your idea."

"What if her idea is different from ours?" Ann asked. "What do we write?"

"Let me tell you what I noticed in other groups. Grace and Jill have one idea while Laura and Teddy have another. Laura is recording for the group, and she is writing about both ideas. It's the same with Chris's group. He and Bayard think one thing, Brandie thinks another, and Andreas thinks still another. Chris is reporting all that."

I stopped talking for a moment. The children were quiet. I added another comment, "What is important is that you work together and discuss your ideas. Sometimes ideas change as you hear from one another, and this is how you learn. Also, you'll want to be sure that what you are writing really tells what people in your group are thinking."

This discussion seemed to help the group process. Patrick read what he had written, and the group talked about it. He inserted some changes and then continued writing.

The group's final paper read: *"We except for Amber think four reds, 5 yellows and three blues is the answer. We think this because on the last pick there were less blues and more reds and yellows. Amber thinks that there are seven blues, two reds and three yellows. Amber thinks this because the fewest number was five for reds and 25 was the most for blues. And three yellows because if you divieded six you would get three."*

Dealing with situations such as this one is essential for helping children to learn to work together. It's worth the time.

Chapter 16
The Place-Value Game

The Place-Value Game relies on a combination of luck and strategy. It is a game that is easy to teach and easy for children to play. The game provides children with the opportunity to learn about the equally likely possibilities of rolling the numbers on one die while reinforcing their understanding of place value.

The goal of this game is to try to make the largest four-digit number possible. Each digit is determined by the roll of a die. Each time the die is rolled, all players write the number that comes up in the ones, tens, hundreds, or thousands place. Once a digit is written, it cannot be changed. The die is rolled five times, allowing each player to reject one roll.

Having the children use the same rolls of the die to play results in as many ties as wins and losses. Having the children write about the strategies they use results in their focusing on their analysis of their experience. Both of these help to deemphasize the aspect of winning, and instead keeps the emphasis of the experience on children's thinking.

INTRODUCING THE LESSON

I introduced the idea of the game to the children by asking them to make a three-digit number using a 1, a 2, and a 3. I listed the numbers they made on the board—123, 132, 321, 312, 213, and 231.

What's the largest number I can make with these three digits?" I asked. They easily identified that it was 321.

"What's the smallest?" I asked. They answered that it was 123.

I next posed a problem to check their understanding. "In your groups," I said, "see if you can figure out the largest and smallest numbers you can make using four digits—a 3, a 2, a 5, and an 8." I wrote these digits on the board.

It was not problematic for the groups to identify 8,532 as the largest and 2,358 as the smallest. This was not an assessment of each child's ability, however. I knew that some children would have difficulty doing this individually. However, I also knew that from playing the game in their groups, they would get many chances to examine numbers and to figure out how they compare.

Then I introduced the children to the game. I drew the following diagram on the board, and directed them to do the same on paper. "Be sure you draw your boxes large enough so that you have room to write a number in each one," I told them.

To play the Place-Value Game, children write numbers in each box in the diagram.

I then gave the rules for playing. "I'm going to roll the die five times," I explained. "Each time I roll, I'll call out the number, and you write it in one of your boxes. Once you write it, you are not allowed to change it. After the five rolls, you'll each have a four-digit number to read and a number in the extra box. The extra box is the reject box. It doesn't count for the number. The idea is to try to place your digits so that you'll end up with the largest number possible."

I played a game with the entire class, rolling the die five times and entering the numbers that came up in my boxes on the board while the children did so on their papers. The children compared their final numbers in their groups to see who had come up with the largest. I asked the person in each group who had the largest to report the number. In this way, I was able to reinforce that I wanted them to read the number properly. The children seemed surprised that the largest numbers differed from group to group.

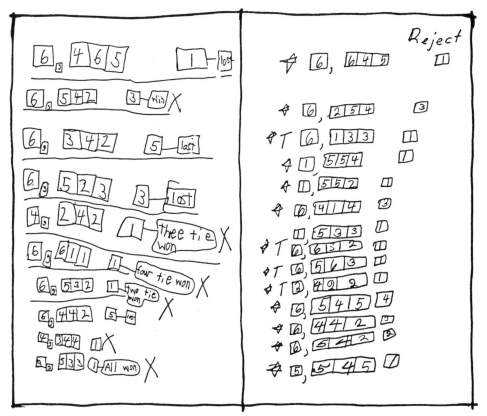

Children use different systems for indicating wins, losses, and ties.

After one child rolls the die, everyone in the group writes the number in a box.

I then explained how they were to play in their groups. "Each group will have a die," I said. "Take turns rolling it. When a number is rolled, everyone in your group needs to write it in one of the boxes before the next person rolls."

The children played the game with enthusiasm. Groups devised their own ways for keeping score. Some put a star next to a winning number. Others marked whether they won, lost, or if it was a tie. Some kept track of wins with tally marks; in the case of ties, each person with the largest number got a mark.

I purposely did not make a worksheet of gameboards for the children. I purposely did not tell them how to keep score, or even if they should keep score. I think that children benefit from the experience of organizing themselves for purposes such as these.

The next day, several of the children reported that they had played the game at home with their parents or brothers and sisters. Their interest was still high.

A CLASS DISCUSSION

After the children had had the opportunity to play the game for several days, I conducted a class discussion. "I'd like to talk with you about the Place-Value Game," I said. "I'm interested in what you've figured out about playing to win."

Hands shot up instantly, and children offered a variety of ideas. "It's a good idea to put a 6 in the first box." "I always put a 1 in the reject box." "I put a 5 or 6 in the thousands place." "You have to decide if you'll take a chance with a 3." I didn't comment or probe their ideas, but merely gave all who wanted to the chance to talk.

"What problems did you find when you were playing the game?" I asked.

Bayard had a thought. "Sometimes you wait for a big number to put in the first box, and then it doesn't come, so you lose."

Teddy had a different problem. "When I roll a 4, I'm not sure what to do with it."

"I don't like it when all little numbers come up," Alana said.

I wrote the word *strategy* on the chalkboard. "Does anyone know what this word, *strategy*, means?" I asked.

Only two children offered to respond. "It's like a plan," Patrick said. "It's a way to win," Jill explained.

"I agree with Patrick and Jill," I said. "A strategy is a plan, in this case a plan for where to write the numbers that come up on the die so you have a good chance of making the largest number possible. All of the ideas you have are parts of a strategy. For example, Grace said that she always puts a 1 in the reject box. How many of you also do that?" Most of the children raised their hands.

"Here's a question I have," I continued. "What do you do with a 1 if there already is a number in the reject box? What is your strategy then?" The children all knew what they would do. They would put it in the ones place.

"What if the ones place already has a number in it?" I asked. I was trying to push them to see that a strategy has a causal aspect to it—if this is the situation, then I'll do that. They weren't terribly interested in considering these possibilities, so I shifted their attention to a writing assignment.

"What I'd like you to do now," I said, "is to write about the strategy you use to play the game. I'm interested in how you're thinking about this, so I want you to write all you can about what you do when you play."

The children got to work enthusiastically. They wrote a great deal. Their involvement with the game, and enjoyment, seemed to give them a lot to report.

Some children used the place-value names for the boxes. Andreas, for example, wrote: *"My strategy is if it is one or two I reject it. If it is six I put it in the thousands box. If it is five I put it in the hundreds box and if it is four I put it in the tens box and if it is three I put it in the ones box."*

Timothy, however, referred to the boxes by their position, not by their place-value names: *"I put two or under in the reject box. Or like if somebody rolls a four I'd put it in the middle box. If they roll a five I'd put it in the second box. If they roll a three I'd put it in the fourth box."*

Timothy Weiss
Oct. 28, 1987

My Strategy

I put two or under in the reject box. Or
Like if somebody rolls a four I'd put it
in the middle box. If they roll a five I'd
put it in the second box. If they roll a
three I'd put it in the fourth box.

Grace Rubenstein
Wed. Oct. 28, 1987

Our table got 9 all ties and
8 all in a row. One of them was all
1s. My stratagy was that if there
was one I put it in the regect
box. I put 6s in the thousands box.
I put 3s in the ones box. I put 4s
in the tens box. I put 5s in
the hundreds box. I never
won alone but I was in a few
winning ties and a few losing ties.
I was dissapointed when I lost
but I know games are for fun
not winning.

Timothy and Grace are specific in their decisions for placing numbers; Grace adds to her strategy a bit of philosophy about winning and losing.

Teddy finds the need to change his strategy after some experience.

> Teddy B [?]
> Oct. 28, 1987
>
> I thought taking chances on low C.
> numbers like 2 is better than putting
> it in the reject box. Thats how I won
> a game. We all almost had the same
> stratege. Thats how we got 9 all ties.
> I lost three games from not taking ___.
> chances. So I changed my stratege. ___

Some children presented ideas separately, without resolving difficulties that could arise. Patrick, for example, didn't notice a problem when he said he would put a one and a two into the reject box. He wrote: *"My strategy was when I rolled the dice I made the six be in the thousands place. And every time there came a one first I put it in the reject box. When I had a five I put it in the hundreds place. Every time I got a three I put it in ones place. And when I had a two I also put it in the reject box."*

Shaney, however, did consider how ideas related to one another. She wrote: *"When I got a 1 I put it in the rejected box relly fast. When I got a 6 I put it in the first box. If I got a 5 if it hadded been used yet I put the 5 in the 2 box. And 4's I put them in the 2ond to the last box. And three I put any where I wanted. Some times I got to be careful. I won 5 times."*

Teddy wrote about his approach to the game in a more general way: *"I thought taking chances on low numbers like 2 is better than putting it in the reject box. Thats how I won a game. We all almost had the same stratege. Thats how we got 9 all ties. I lost three games from not taking chances. So I changed my stratege."*

Grace was in the same group as Teddy: *"Our table got 9 all ties and 8 all in a row. One of them was all 1s. My stratagy was that if there was one I put it in the regect box. I put 6s in the thousands box. I put 3s in the ones box. I put 4s in the tens box. I put 5s in the hundreds box. I never won alone but I was in a few winning ties and a few losing ties. I was dissapointed when I lost but I know games are for fun not winning."*

Michelle learned something about the realities of probability: *"I put the highest number in the thousand box (the first box.) That was usaully 6. I put the lowest number in the reject box. That was usaully 1. Our groop tied a lot. Most of the time I tied in first or second place. Sometimes I lost because someone called five and I put it in the seccond box because we usally called six, but sometimes they didn't and I lost."*

Chapter 17
A Probability Menu

The Probability Menu provides children with a collection of experiences that help develop understanding of several important mathematical ideas. Children learn that some outcomes are more likely than others and investigate why. They learn that gathering data can be helpful for testing predictions or hypotheses. They learn to use a representative sample of data to make inferences. Their learning occurs from engaging in experiments and analyzing the results.

As well as contributing to their understanding of probability, these activities also help develop children's sense of number. In Tiles in the Bags, children make use of the idea of ratio in an informal way. Two-Spinner Sums and the Game of Pig provide practice with basic addition facts and sums to 100. The Subtraction Game not only provides subtraction practice, but also has them consider what affects the size of differences between numbers.

In addition, the activities provide experience with different ways to collect data. The Spinner Experiment, Two-Spinner Sums, and Shake and Spill structure the data collection for the children. In the other experiments, children have the responsibility for organizing the data they collect so that they can then make sense of the information.

BEFORE THE MENU—INTRODUCTORY ACTIVITIES

Several lessons preceded the children's work on the menu tasks. These lessons were designed to prepare the children in two ways. They provided children with a base of experience with some of the concepts in the menu activities on which they could build understanding. Also, the introductory lessons prepared the children for the logistics of some of the menu activities, which avoided overwhelming them with too many directions and new materials.

In one introductory lesson, the children made spinners, used them for individual experiments, and then collectively analyzed the results from the entire class. This activity helped prepare the children for Two-Spinner Sums. The introductory spinner lesson was similar to the one done with second graders in Chapter 14.

In another introductory lesson, the children learned a game that linked place-value understanding with probability. Learning this game taught the children the convention they would use for playing the Subtraction Game and provided them with a beginning opportunity to think about using a strategy. A description of this lesson appears in Chapter 16.

Also in preparation for the menu, children participated in a lesson in which they were asked to predict what Color Tiles were in a bag. This was a sampling experience in which children collected data that they used to make their predictions. This activity is described in Chapter 15.

It is important to note that these preparatory experiences do not have to precede the menu work immediately. Children benefit from time to digest experiences before coming back to the same ideas in other ways. The firmer their base of understanding, the more profitable the connections they make among activities. Additional experiences then serve to help children sort out and refine their thoughts and further internalize their understanding.

PREPARING FOR THE MENU

The menu consisted of five activities. In preparation, I made seven folders, one for each group of children. Folders were made from 12-inch-by-18-inch pieces of construction paper folded in half. I stapled a list of the menu tasks on the left-hand side inside each folder and the directions for the five tasks on the right-hand side. I also included a recording sheet for Two-Spinner Sums and four recording sheets for Shake and Spill.

I made an extra copy of the activities and recording sheets to use when I introduced the tasks to the class. In addition, I collected the materials the children would need—dice, spinners with the numbers 0 through 9 on them, two-color counters that are red on one side and yellow on the other, three lunch bags, nine red tiles, thirteen blue tiles, and fourteen yellow tiles to fill the bags. I also colored a sample for each possibility from the two-color counter activity to post on the chalkboard for Shake and Spill.

The preparation took me about two hours. Though it was time-consuming, the preparation time didn't seem excessive when I realized that the children would be working on the menu for more than a week.

Unlike the Place-Value menu described in Chapter 7, these activities were not set up in different parts of the room. All the materials were kept in a central location. Children went there and got what they needed as they worked.

INTRODUCING THE MENU

Explaining the menu to the class and modeling what they were to do took almost an entire class period. It is valuable to take this time. The better the children understand what it is they are to do, the more easily they can concentrate on what each activity has to offer, rather than get bogged down with logistic details.

I called the children to the rug for the introduction, pulling them in close to explain what they would be doing. I find that this closeness helps me keep the children's attention for a longer time. Also, there is a bulletin board next to the rug area where I could post the menu tasks, and a counter where I could put all the materials.

The children gather on the rug to be introduced to the menu activities.

"I have prepared five different activities for you to do in your groups," I began. "Today, I'm going to teach you how to do them. I've listed the activities on a menu for you." I posted the list of activities.

"First on the menu is Two-Spinner Sums," I continued. "Let me tell you about that. This is a spinner experiment that differs from the one you did last week with the 1-2-3 spinner. in this experiment, you use spinners that have the numbers 0 through 9 on them, each with the same amount of space. I've made two spinners to show you what you are to do. I've also made new spinner faces that you can cut out and exchange with the faces on the spinners you made last week. We'll keep all the spinners in this box."

I posted a copy of the directions for this activity along with a sample recording sheet. "In this experiment, you spin two spinners and mark the sum that comes up on the recording sheet," I explained. I gave a spinner to Jill and one to Timmy and asked that they spin and report what numbers came up. Jill got a 7; Timmy got a 4.

"Think about how much seven plus four is," I said, and waited a moment. "Let's say the answer together. How much is seven and four?" The children answered "eleven" in a chorus.

I showed them how to mark the sum with an X on the recording sheet, and then repeated this procedure two more times. It seemed straightforward to the children.

"When you do this activity," I explained further, "first, discuss and write as a group which sums you think will come up most often and which you think will come up least often. That is step one on the directions. Step two says to do the experiment, spinning and adding until one sum reaches the top. Step three tells you to describe your graph, as we've done for other graphs. Step four asks you to record on the class chart the sum that reached the top." I posted a piece of ditto paper for this step.

"Any questions?" I asked. There were none.

"Next is the Subtraction Game," I continued. You play this game as you do the Place-Value Game, filling in boxes with numbers. In this game, however, you'll use the 0–9 spinner instead of a die. After four spins, you subtract, and the person with the smallest answer wins."

I posted the directions and an additional sheet on which I showed the children how to draw the boxes for the game. This time I did the spinning and had volunteers tell me where they would put each number. After spinning a 1, a 6, an 8, and a 2, I had this problem.

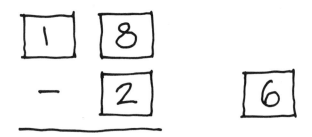

"How much is eighteen minus two?" I asked. Again, I had them answer as a class, and I recorded sixteen.

Patrick raised his hand. "If the eight was where the two is and the two was where the eight is, the answer would be only four." I drew another set of boxes and had Patrick come up and write the numbers where he had suggested. The class agreed that his idea was better.

"But remember," I reminded the class, "once you write a number, you can't change it. Play at least ten games in your group, and then write about your strategies. You'll do this writing individually, not as a group."

I was comfortable that the children understood this game, and continued with the next activity. "Next is Tiles in the Bags," I said, and posted the activity.

"Is that like what we did before?" Marina asked.

"Yes," I answered, "but with a new twist. This time I filled three bags with tiles. Each bag has twelve tiles in it. As it says on the directions, one has six red, three blue, and three yellow tiles. One has two red, eight blue, and two yellow. The other has one red, two blue, and nine yellow. But you don't know which bag has which contents. Your job is to find out. Choose one bag and take samples, just as we've done before. Then predict what's in the bag, and finally you get to peek."

Michelle
Nov. 6, 1987

Strategy for Subtraction
My strategy was to put
the bigest number in the
'take' away box. I put
the lowest number in the
first box, so I could take
away a big number like
9 from a small number.

AnnMacdonald
Nov. 10, 1987

Tiles in a bag
I think that the answer is 2 red and
8 blue, and 2 yellow. I think this
because blue came up alot in each
time we tried and red and yellow
came up the least each time we
tried so I looked at the chart we were
soposed to diside the answer from
and the one whith the most blue was
the one whith 8 blue, two red
and two yellow. So I decided
that mast be the answer.

Michelle explains her strategy for the Subtraction Game; Ann makes a prediction for Tiles in a Bag.

"Any questions?" I asked.

"How many times do we have to do it before we can look?" Michael asked.

"The directions tell you to take twelve samples, and to do that three times," I responded. "Remember to check the directions when you work." I felt confident that the children could do this game because we had done sampling from tiles in a bag several times before.

I went on to the next activity. "Next is the Game of Pig. I think the best way to explain it is to play a game. Who would like to play with me?" I chose Teddy and Kendra, and they came over to the counter where I was.

I posted three sheets of paper, one for Teddy, one for Kendra, and one for me. "The idea of the game," I explained, "is to get to 100. You take turns rolling two dice, adding in your head the numbers that come up. When one person is rolling, everyone should help with the adding. Your turn can be as long as you like. But, here's the catch. If you roll a 1, your turn is over and you score 0 that round. And if two 1s come up on the dice, your whole score goes back to 0."

> **Kendra**
>
> Astradigy
>
> I think that if you roll a good number that if you go agein You will probaly get a one.
>
> So you better not be a pig!

> **Teddy**
>
> My strateggy is taking chances but you don't want to take chances in this game. Thats how I lost 8 out of 10.

Kendra and Teddy offer advice for playing the Game of Pig.

Timothy

I would just think it over. If I thought I would get a one or a double one I would stick. But if I thought I would get a one or a double one I wouldn't stick.

Stertigy

Mairead 5?
Nov 6 1987

I had 99 but Gabe won. He had 94 but he got ten and won by four. My Stertigy was to pray for no ones. But last roll of all I got a one.

Kendra went first. She called out the numbers, and the class added together. On her third roll, she rolled a 1. There were groans of sympathy. I recorded 0 on her paper.

Teddy went next. He rolled a 1 on his first roll, and I recorded a 0. More groans of sympathy.

Then I went. I rolled a 7 and a 4 and decided to stop. I wrote 11 on my paper.

We continued in this fashion. Teddy never got off the ground. He kept rolling 1s on his first, second, or third rolls. At one point, he changed the dice for another pair, but that didn't help.

Kendra's score and mine kept pretty close, though we each experienced our mishaps. The children were definitely rooting for Kendra, and she did win, though I wasn't far behind. There was much cheering.

Bayard had a question. "Is it okay for your score to go over 100?" he asked. I answered that it was fine, that whoever got to 100 or more first was the winner.

"After you play five games," I added, "you are to write about your strategy individually."

I then settled the children to explain the fifth activity. I posted the directions for Shake and Spill, and demonstrated what they were to do with the two-color counters. For this demonstration, I passed out six counters to ten children.

"In a moment," I explained, "you each will shake and spill the six counters and call out what came up. First, report how many red, and then how many yellow." I did the task once for the children.

"While they are doing this," I said, "the rest of you listen carefully. I'm going to ask you which combinations were called out most often and which were called out least often."

The children did as I had instructed them. When I stopped them, the children reported that they had heard "three and three" and "four and two" and "two and four" most often.

"We hardly heard six of anything," Michelle said.

"For this activity," I explained, "you each will shake and spill six counters and record what comes up each time by coloring in a recording sheet." I posted a sample sheet and continued. "After doing this activity six times, cut your recording sheet into six separate experiments and post each where it belongs on the class graph I've set up." I had posted a column of one of each possibility on the chalkboard.

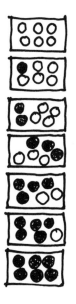

"Post them neatly so they line up one underneath the other," I said. "That way we can more easily compare how many of each combination came up. When the class graph is complete, your group is to write everything you notice about the results."

"What questions do you have?" I asked.

"Why do you call it a menu?" Andreas asked.

"Because it is a list of what's available," I explained, "just like a restaurant menu is a list. You don't get to choose what you do on this menu, but you do get to choose the order in which your group will do them. You can start with any one you like. Also, you don't do the "dessert" activity until you have completed all the others."

"You didn't tell us about the dessert," Grace said.

"If you have completed all the activities and there is still time to work, you can play the Place-Value Game you've learned," I explained.

"Can we start now?" Gabe asked.

"There are just a few minutes until recess," I said, "so you can start after that. But first let me show you the folders you'll use." I showed the children how all the directions were stapled inside the group folders. I showed them how to color in the box next to each task listed on the menu when they had completed it.

I gave one final direction. "When you return from recess, the first thing your group is to do is to choose an activity. The second thing is to have someone in your group read the directions aloud, starting with what's written in the box at the top. Then you can get organized and begin."

I distributed the folders and had the children return to their desks and get ready for recess.

It was a lot of explaining for me and a lot of listening for the children. The children did well, however. Involving them in spinning the spinners and playing the games helped keep their attention.

WORKING ON THE MENU

The children worked on the menu for the next eight math periods. My major role in the first two days was to make sure they were doing all parts of each activity. The children plunged into the activities with gusto, but had to be reminded about the writing assignments. Because I had done a great deal of writing with these children, it was now a natural extension of their math work, so keeping them on task was not very difficult.

Before we started each math period, I had a class discussion to talk about how their work was progressing. This gave me the opportunity to remind the children that their job was not to race to finish the tasks, but to do each one carefully. I also reminded them to return materials and keep them orderly.

Also during this time, children were asked to bring up any problems they encountered that they thought the group should think about. Chris, for example, said, "Sometimes we have trouble agreeing on which activity to do next. Can we work separately?"

His question gave me a chance to talk about working together as a group. I asked how other groups decided which task to do next. There were several suggestions.

"We take turns deciding," Alana reported for her group.

"We're just doing them in the order on the menu," Shaney said.

"Perhaps these suggestions will help," I told Chris's group.

Andreas reported a snag while playing the subtraction game. He was in a group with Erika and Tara. In one game, the four numbers that came up on the spinner were 0, 1, 3, and 7. Andreas had placed his numbers to get:

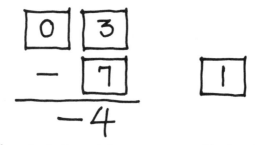

"I didn't know how to do three take away seven," he said, "so I figured out it could be minus four. But we still don't know whose answer was the smallest." I was surprised by this, both by how he solved the subtraction problem and by the group's confusion over which number was smallest. I asked how Tara and Erika had placed the numbers. They both came to the board to show what they had done:

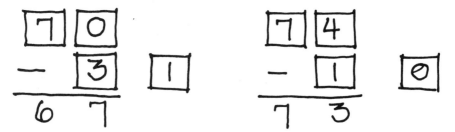

"Which is smallest?" Andreas asked. This was one of those rare but wonderful instances in a classroom; I never could have predicted such a dilemma. I asked if anyone in the class had an idea. Marina did.

"I think minus four is the smallest," she said, "because it's less than zero, like four below zero."

Andreas was not convinced and looked to me for confirmation. "I agree with Marina," I said. Andreas broke into a huge grin.

"An answer such as minus four," I said, "is sometimes called negative four. As Marina said, negative numbers are smaller than zero. You'll learn more about those kinds of numbers when you get into the sixth or seventh grade." The children seemed impressed.

OBSERVING THE CHILDREN AT WORK

While the children worked, I circulated, answered questions, gave help to groups as needed, and observed and listened to the children while they worked. Organizational problems in groups arose from time to time. For example, I noticed Vanessa and Amber playing the Game of Pig as Patrick and Ann, the other members in their group, were doing Two-Spinner Sums. I reminded them that they were to work together on one task so that they could discuss with one another what they were doing and learning.

Another group, with Chris, Bayard, Brandie, and Jason, was doing the dessert activity before finishing the others. Although they were very involved with the Place-Value Game, I interrupted them and directed them back to the required activities.

At another time, Gabe reported a problem he was having with Nick. The group was playing the Subtraction Game. "I did my subtraction," he said, "and Nick said I did it wrong. But we both got the same answer, so I don't think I'm wrong." He showed me his paper and how he had subtracted eight from twelve, carefully borrowing and performing the standard algorithm. He had written:

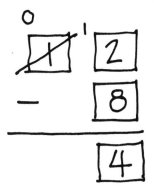

Nick's comment was, "You don't have to borrow. You just subtract and get the answer."

"That's the way I know how," Gabe said, defending his work.

"I think they're both right," Mairead chimed in.

"I agree with Mairead," I said. "I think what Nick is saying is that you could have done the problem without regrouping. Do you know how much thirteen minus five is, Gabe?"

Gabe thought for a minute and then said, "Eight."

"That's right," I said. "I can write the problem and the answer without doing any regrouping. Look." I recorded it and continued, "I could regroup, but I don't need to. I think it's a good idea to look at a problem to see if you can use your head first to get the answer before using your pencil. But either way is okay."

The thought came to me that after the children were involved playing a game such as this one would be a good time to teach or review how to regroup for subtraction. The teaching of skills is best done when a need for that skill has been established, and this situation created a need.

EXTENDING THE MENU

Each of the activities has the potential to lead to further investigations. I added some of these extensions to the menu. Thus, groups that finished first could stay involved, while others needed more time.

The class graph for Shake and Spill grows as children post their results from tossing six two-color counters.

One extension related to the Game of Pig. From reading through the strategies the children were writing, I found most were describing what happened rather than what they were thinking. I thought they might benefit from another way to look at the game, and introduced a group graph on which they were all to record before they got to work one day.

I wrote the numbers from 1 to 20 on the board in two columns. Above them I wrote: How Many Rolls to Get a 1? Then I demonstrated what the children were to do.

"I'm going to roll two dice until a 1 comes up on at least one of them," I explained. "I'm also going to count to see on which roll it happens." I did two and made a tally mark next to the numbers 2 and 3 to indicate how many rolls it took each time to get a 1.

Then I passed the dice to one group and had each child roll until a 1 came up. I recorded their results as well.

"I'm interested in having you see what happens if this is done many times," I then said, "so I'd like you each to do this experiment once over the next few days. Those of you who have finished all the menu activities can do

For Andreas, the value of playing the Game of Pig extends beyond his mathematics learning.

> **Pig**
>
> Andreas Stringer
> Nov. 13,1987
>
> Pig is my favorite activity because I like doing games that use dice. And also I like adding. It helped me add and it helped me to lose with out being unfair and geting mad.

it more times to add to our information." This activity gave them another opportunity to have information to consider when thinking about a situation.

Another extension was an art activity. The children were learning about colors in science, and knew the difference between primary and secondary colors. I showed them how to divide a spinner face into eighths and color them with two alternating primary colors—red and yellow, blue and yellow, or red and blue. They were to predict what color they would see when they spun the spinner. Several groups did this activity, using the reverse side of the spinners they had already made.

A third extension was Two-Dice Sums, an activity similar to Two-Spinner Sums. I was interested in seeing what connections, if any, they would make between these two activities.

SUMMARIZING THE MENU

From checking their folders, I could ascertain which tasks had been done by the children. When an activity had been completed by all groups, I took time to discuss it, having the children report their reactions and strategies, offering further ideas where appropriate.

For example, I had the groups read what they had recorded about the Shake and Spill graph. One group had included a section describing Grace's idea. Michael read, *"Grace predicted 3 and 3 because there is a 50% chance that it will be red. There is a 50% chance that it will be yellow. That means that it will usually be 3 and 3. That prediction was right."*

Subtraction Game

Amber Rosenbaum
Nov. 5, 1997

I like the subtraction game because it was mistierieously fun. You coulden't see who was ahead like in Candy Land. It was like the evidintce was coverd up. It realy made you think. and it was exiting.

My stratige was that if I got a nine. I would put it in the box that you were suposed to subtract from, becuase nine is the hyist number and the more you subtract the more less you end up with.

Amber's favorite activity on the Probability menu is the Subtraction Game.

I asked the children if others had ideas about why three and three came up so often and why all red and all yellow came up so rarely. Children offered different ideas. After this discussion, I gave the class an individual writing assignment to answer two questions: (1) Why did three red and three yellow come up more often than other combinations? (2) Why did all red and all yellow come up fewer times?

Laura wrote: "*1. I think 3 and 3 came up the most because there is more of a chance. 2. I think all yellow and all red came up so few because it is hard for them all at the same time to flip to the same side. And there is not as much chance as the other one.*"

Shaney wrote: "*1. I think that 3 and 3 came up the most because there are 6 two color counters and each of them have red and yellow on each side. So if you spill the counters there is a 50 prsent that you will get 3 reds and a 50 present that you will get 3 yellow. 2. I think that you don't get all yellow or all red because when you throw the counters it will mostly come out to be some yellow and some red. But sometimes it will come out all red or all yellow but not usaly. It did not work for me!*"

Michelle's reasoning was in part mathematically abstract and in part concrete: "*1. Three red and three yellow came up the most because the two-colored counters have red on one side and yellow on the other side and like Grace said, there is 50 percent of a chance yellow will come up and 50 percent of a chance red will come up. Another reason three and three came up the most is that the two-colored counters flip around in the air and twist and twirl on the table so they land on the table three red and three yellow. 2. All red and all yellow came up fewer times because the two-colored counters have red on one side and yellow on the other so each two colored counter uasaully lands on difrent colors so all red and all yellow came up fewer times.*"

Bryce, a shy boy socially and intellectually, had a more terse response: "*1. I think red and yellow two color counters came out even because they are even. 2. It is very unsherwul to get every coler the same.*"

It is important to keep in mind that I had no goal of mastery for the menu activities. Instead, my goal was for children to enjoy this mathematical experience. I wanted to stimulate their intellectual curiosity and nurture their understanding of mathematical ideas. I realize that while one activity might spark initial learning for some children, it may extend or cement existing understanding for others. Children learn in their own ways, at their own paces. My evaluation consists of learning to see what each child now understands so that I can provide further instructional opportunities that are rich enough to keep each child involved and growing.

These are the directions the children use for the Probability menu.

PROBABILITY MENU

Names _____
_____
_____
_____

Color in the box to show when you have completed a task.

Keep all work in your group's folder.

☐ Two-Spinner Sums
☐ The Subtraction Game
☐ Tiles in the Bags
☐ The Game of Pig
☐ Shake and Spill

DESSERT

☐ The Place-Value Game

The Subtraction Game

In this game, the object is to get the smallest answer you can. You play it as you do the Place-Value Game, placing numbers in boxes. Then you subtract and see who has the smallest answer.

You need : a 0-9 spinner

① Draw the boxes for the game. (The box on the side is a reject box.)

② Take turns spinning the spinner. Each player writes the number that came up in a box. (Once it is written, it can't be moved.) After four spins, subtract and compare your answers.

③ Play at least 10 games. You need to play enough times to figure out a strategy.

④ Write your strategy for winning. (Each write your own strategy.)

Tiles in a Bag

There are 12 tiles in each bag. They are red, blue, and yellow. Different numbers of each color are in each bag. Your task is to take one bag and, <u>without looking inside</u>, predict its contents.

① Take one bag. Record whether it is A, B, or C.

② Without looking <u>inside</u>, reach in and take out one tile. Record its color. Then put it back in the bag and shake the bag to mix the tiles. Do this 12 times.

③ Repeat step ② two more times.

④ Now, still without looking, predict whether you think the bag has :

   6 red, 3 blue, 3 yellow OR
   2 red, 8 blue, 2 yellow OR
   1 red, 2 blue, 9 yellow

Explain your prediction.

⑤ Finally, check your prediction by looking. Then put the bag for another group to use.

The Game of Pig

The winner of The Game of Pig is the person who gets to 100 first. You do this by rolling two dice and adding the numbers that come up. But there is danger!

You need: 2 dice

Rules :

① Take turns. On your turn, you roll the dice as many times as you want, adding what comes up in your head.

② If a 1 comes up on <u>one</u> of the dice, you lose all you got on that turn and the next player goes.

③ If a 1 comes up on <u>both</u> dice, your total goes back to 0 and the next player goes.

④ If you stop rolling before a 1 comes up, write your score down and add it to your total.

⑤ Play at least five games. Then write about your strategy. (Do this individually.)

Two-Spinner Sums

If you spin two 0-9 spinners, and add the numbers that come up, there are 19 possible sums:

0, 1, 2, 3, 4, 5, ... , 16, 17, 18

In this activity, you investigate if some sums come up more or less often than others.

You need: 2 0-9 spinners
Two-Spinner Sum
recording sheets.

① Discuss and then write your group's predictions about these two questions:

1. Which sum (or sums) will come up most often?
2. Which sum (or sums) will come up least often?

② Spin the spinners. Record the sum until one sum reaches the top.

③ Describe your graph. Write complete sentences.

④ Record which sum reached the top on the class chart.

Shake and Spill

In this activity, you shake and spill 6 two-color counters, coloring in on the recording sheet how many reds and yellows come up. We'll collect everyone's information on a class graph.

You need: 6 two-color counters
a recording sheet

① Each person shakes and spills 6 two-color counters. Record with crayons on the recording sheet.

② Repeat this 5 more times.

③ Cut your recording sheet into 6 separate pieces. Post them on the class graph.

④ When the class graph is complete, write (as a group) all that you notice about the results posted

TWO-SPINNER SUMS
Recording Sheet

| 0 | 1 | 2 | 3 | 4 | 5 | 6 | 7 | 8 | 9 | 10 | 11 | 12 | 13 | 14 | 15 | 16 | 17 | 18 |

What Now?

These lessons grew out of many hours of collaboration. Just as children's learning is supported when they have the chance to interact and exchange ideas, so was our learning and understanding supported through working together. It was a special opportunity to share teaching ideas, make plans for lessons together, watch each other teach, rehash what occurred, and discuss what we might try next.

We know how difficult it is for classroom teachers to have the opportunity for the kind of collaboration we experienced while developing the lessons and writing this book. However, we encourage you to find support from your colleagues. In that spirit, we invite you to use the following questions to analyze the lessons in this book so that you may better use them as springboards for your own thinking and teaching.

1. In what ways does the lesson promote students' mathematical thinking and reasoning?

2. What concepts and skills were presented in the lesson?

3. Where would such a lesson fit in your math program?

4. How does your current textbook provide for instruction in this area?

5. How could the lesson be improved?

6. How would you have responded differently in one or more instances?

7. What changes would you make to teach this lesson to your class?

8. What effect do you think the activities in the lesson can have on students' attitudes toward math?

We hope you will approach the lessons in this book with the same spirit of problem solving that the lessons promote. There is no one right or best way to help children learn mathematics, just as there is no one right way to approach solving a math problem. We encourage you to make these lessons yours, learn with your children, and enjoy your mathematical explorations.

INDEX